Anonymus

Intermediate Education Board for Ireland report

1895

Anonymus

Intermediate Education Board for Ireland report
1895

ISBN/EAN: 9783742801289

Manufactured in Europe, USA, Canada, Australia, Japa

Cover: Foto ©ninafisch / pixelio.de

Manufactured and distributed by brebook publishing software
(www.brebook.com)

Anonymus

Intermediate Education Board for Ireland report

REPORT

OF THE

INTERMEDIATE EDUCATION BOARD

FOR IRELAND

FOR THE YEAR 1895.

Presented to both Houses of Parliament by Command of Her Majesty.

DUBLIN:
PRINTED FOR HER MAJESTY'S STATIONERY OFFICE,
BY ALEXANDER THOM & CO. (LIMITED), ABBEY-STREET.

And to be purchased, either directly or through any Bookseller, from
HODGES, FIGGIS, & CO. (LIMITED), 104, GRAFTON-STREET, DUBLIN; or
EYRE & SPOTTISWOODE, EAST HARDING-STREET, FLEET-STREET, E.C.; or
JOHN MENZIES & CO., 12, HANOVER-STREET, EDINBURGH,
and 90, WEST NILE-STREET, GLASGOW.

1896.

[C.—8034.] *Price 6½d.*

CONTENTS.

REPORT

OF THE

INTERMEDIATE EDUCATION BOARD

FOR IRELAND

FOR THE YEAR 1895.

TO HIS EXCELLENCY, GEORGE HENRY,
EARL CADOGAN, K.G.,

LORD LIEUTENANT GENERAL AND GENERAL GOVERNOR OF IRELAND.

MAY IT PLEASE YOUR EXCELLENCY,

We, the Commissioners of Intermediate Education (Ireland), submit to your Excellency this our Sixteenth Report.

The number of students who gave notice of their intention to present for examination in 1895 was:—

Boys.	Girls.	Total.
6,753	2,263	9,016

being an increase of 476, or 7·6 per cent., in the case of boys and an increase of 106, or 0·4 per cent., in the case of girls; and a total increase of 8 per cent. on the corresponding numbers in 1894; and a total increase of 18·9 per cent. on the corresponding numbers in 1893.

In the ten last years the numbers were:—

Year.	Boys.	Girls.	Total.
1886	4,681	1,348	6,029
1887	5,018	1,460	6,477
1888	4,963	[illegible]	6,589
1889	5,561	1,578	7,139
1890	5,311	1,458	6,769
1891	4,196	1,441	5,637
1892	4,714	1,622	6,336
1893	5,730	1,856	7,586
1894	6,379	2,067	8,446
1895	6,765	2,253	9,018

See Table 1. The number of students who presented themselves for examination in 1895 was:—

Boys.	Girls.	Total.
6,267	2,055	8,322

being an increase of 451 or 7·7 per cent. in the case of boys, and an increase of 190 or 10·2 per cent. in the case of girls, and a total increase of 641 or 8·4 per cent. on the corresponding numbers in 1894

In the ten last years the numbers were:—

Year.	Boys.	Girls.	Total.
1886, . .	4,443	1,105	5,548
1887, . .	4,818	1,216	6,034
1888, . .	4,551	1,507	6,058
1889, . .	4,938	1,595	6,533
1890, . .	3,948	1,198	5,146
1891, . .	3,856	1,300	5,156
1892, . .	4,294	1,465	5,759
1893, . .	5,265	1,709	6,974
1894, . .	5,816	1,865	7,681
1895, . .	6,267	2,055	8,322

See Appendix. The examinations for 1895, which commenced on 17th June and extended over eleven days, were held at 244 centres, in 85 different localities.

The following Table shows the distribution of Centres between the Four Provinces :—

Centres.	Leinster.	Ulster.	Munster.	Connaught.	Totals.
Centres for Boys, .	78	35	56	10	175
Centres for Girls, .	[illegible]	30	11	3	69
Total, . .	97	63	67	13	244

One hundred and eighty gentlemen and seventy ladies were employed as Centre Superintendents, being an average of one Superintendent to every 35 boys and 20 girls examined, respectively.

The number of students who passed the Examinations in 1895 was :— See Table III.

Boys.	Girls.	Total.
3,783	1,190	4,973

In the ten last years the numbers were :—

—	Boys.	Girls.	Total.
1886, .	2,695	595	3,510
1887, .	2,636	909	3,545
1888, .	2,871	1,223	4,094
1889, .	2,844	1,174	4,018
1890, .	2,353	767	3,120
1891, .	2,304	774	3,078
1892, .	2,519	784	3,303
1893, .	3,041	955	3,996
1894, .	3,419	1,104	4,523
1895, .	3,783	1,190	4,973

The proportion *per cent.* of those examined who passed in 1895 was :—

Boys.	Girls.	Boys and Girls.
60·4	57·8	59·6

The proportions in the ten last years were as follows:—

—	Boys.	Girls.	Boys and Girls.
1886, .	61·6	68·6	63·3
1887, .	58·9	78·5	60·
1888, .	63·1	81·1	67·3
1889, .	58·7	69·5	61·5
1890, .	56·1	59·0	56·2
1891, .	55·7	59·3	56·0
1892, .	56·1	53·5	57·7
1893, .	57·7	55·0	57·3
1894, .	58·8	59·2	58·9
1895, .	60·4	57·9	59·6

Exclusive of over-age students the proportion *per cent.* of those examined who passed was:—

Boys.	Girls.	Boys and Girls.
62·2	59·3	61·5

Exclusive of over-age students the proportions in the four last years were as follows:—

Year.	Boys.	Girls.	Boys and Girls.
1892, .	60·4	53·8	57·9
1893, .	59·5	57·8	59·
1894, .	60·3	59·8	60·2
1895, .	62·2	59·3	61·5

See Table V. The number of students to whom were awarded £50 Prizes (Senior Grade), and Exhibitions in the Middle, Junior, and Preparatory Grades was:—

Boys, 359; Girls, 115; Total, 474.

See Table VI. The number of students to whom were awarded prizes in books was—

Boys, 398; Girls, 143; Total, 541.

See Table VII. The number of students to whom were awarded Prizes for Composition under Rule 51 was:—

Boys, 90; Girls, 42; Total, 132.

The number of students to whom were awarded Commercial Prizes under Rule 48 was :— See Table VIII.

Boys, 17 ; Girls, none.

The number of students to whom were awarded Special Money Prizes in lieu of Medals under Rule 49 was :—

Boys, 1 ; Girls, 3 ; Total, 4.

The amount of Results Fees paid to Managers of Schools on account of the Examinations in 1895 was :— See Appendix IV.

Boys, £43,037 13s. 6d. ; Girls, £11,830 7s. 6d. ;

Total, £54,868 1s. 0d.

Of the students, 4,973, who passed the Examination, Results Fees were paid on 4,670, being an average Fee of £11 15s. 0d. per student.

The following Table shows the distribution of Results Fees between the Four Provinces, and the number of Schools in each Province, to the Managers of which Results Fees were paid :—

PROVINCES.	Amount of Results Fees paid.		TOTAL.	No. of Schools.		TOTAL.
	Boys.	Girls.		Boys.	Girls.	
	£ s. d.	£ s. d.	£ s. d.			
LEINSTER,	16,987 9 9	4,234 6 0	21,221 15 9	78	51	129
ULSTER,	9,379 17 0	5,219 19 3	14,599 16 3	56	64	120
MUNSTER,	11,459 8 3	1,956 10 6	13,415 18 9	58	21	79
CONNAUGHT,	1,600 18 6	629 11 9	2,230 10 3	15	5	20
Grand Total,	43,037 13 6	11,830 7 6	54,868 1 0	201	141	342

The values of the Burke Memorial Prizes awarded in 1895 were :— See Table XI., and App. V.

Boys—	Girls—
First Prize, £14 13s. 4d.	Prize, £9 3s. 4d.
Second Prize, £9 3s. 4d.	

FINANCE.

Our Balance Sheet for the year 1895, in respect of the original Endowment (Table IX. *infra*), shows a surplus of £8,078 7s. 1d. (including a sum of £1,083 6s. 8d., Income Tax, to be refunded by the Commissioners of Inland Revenue).

The Local Taxation Account (see Table X.) shows that the Receipts under the Local Taxation (Customs and Excise) Act, and as interest on securities, amounted to £43,308 14s. 10d., and that the expenditure from that account on Results Fees and Exhibitions for 1895 was £55,524 12s. 1d., the excess of expenditure over income, £12,100 17s. 3d., having been met from the amount held in reserve from previous years.

It will thus be seen that the time has arrived to which we looked forward in the framing of our Regulations for the expenditure of the Local Taxation Fund.

As it was obvious that this expenditure would be progressive for some years, our Regulations were necessarily framed in such a way as not to exhaust the entire income in any one of the early years of the working of the Scheme.

It is to be observed that in 1895, taking both accounts into consideration, our total expenditure has exceeded our income from all sources by £9,082 10s. 2d.

A further withdrawal from the amount (Local Taxation Account) held in reserve may be confidently anticipated in the year 1896, and again in 1897, though in the Rules for that year it has been found necessary to reduce the rates of Results Fees in the Preparatory and Junior Grades.

The last payment under the guarantee of the Treasury of interest at 3½ per cent. on our original endowment of £1,000,000 will be made in the year 1896. A serious reduction of the income from the original endowment may then be expected, which will render it necessary to place an increased proportion of charges on the Local Taxation Account.

EDUCATION.

The conditions of passing the examination generally were practically identical with those in force in 1894; the percentage however, of Boys of the prescribed age examined who passed rose, from 60·3 per cent. in that year, to 62·2 per cent. in 1895.

In the case of Girls of the prescribed age there was a slight fall, from 59·9 per cent. in 1894, to 59·3 in 1895.

With regard to the Commercial side of our examinations the number of students qualified for Commercial Certificates was 69 (68 Boys and 1 Girl), compared with 78 (76 Boys and 2 Girls) in 1894.

The number, however, of Special Commercial Prizes gained rose from sixteen in 1894 to seventeen in 1895, although in the latter year students who retained Exhibitions were not eligible for such Prizes.

In addition to these students, many others, as in 1894, who did not aim at obtaining Commercial Certificates, availed themselves of the opportunity of presenting themselves for examination in certain Commercial subjects.

Detailed information respecting the answering of students, Boys and Girls, in the different subjects will be found in the Extracts from the Reports of the Examiners, copies of which were transmitted to all Managers of Schools in Ireland to whom Results Fees were paid in 1895.

TABLE I.—Showing the Number of Students who presented themselves for Examination in the years 1886, 1887, 1888, 1889, 1890, 1891, 1892, 1893, 1894, and 1895.

	Preparatory Grade.									
Year,	1886.	1887.	1888.	1889.	1890.	1891.	1892.	1893.	1894.	1895.
Boys, . . .	–	–	–	–	–	–	1,479	1,773	2,170	2,305
Girls, . . .	–	–	–	–	–	–	391	492	474	619
Total, . .	–	–	–	–	–	–	1,870	2,265	2,644	2,924

TABLE I.—Showing the Number of Students who presented
1889, 1890, 1891, 1892, 1893,

	JUNIOR GRADE.									
YEAR,	1886.	1887.	1888.	1889.	1890.	1891.	1892.	1893.	1894.	1895.
Boys—of the prescribed age, .	3,411	3,627	3,587	3,572	3,070	3,064	3,177	3,497	7,4[illegible]	[illegible]
Do., Over-age, . .	103	61	129	101	94	107	–	[illegible]	[illegible]	[illegible]
Total, . . .	3,517	3,738	3,716	3,673	3,164	3,171	3,177	[illegible]	[illegible]	[illegible]
Girls—of the prescribed age, .	[illegible]	864	1,105	1,927	990	941	788	798	891	[illegible]
Do., Over-age, . .	14	8	11	17	18	15	–	69	[illegible]	[illegible]
Total, . . .	[illegible]	872	1,116	1,944	833	956	788	857	973	1,011
Grand Total, . .	4,400	4,740	4,829	5,317	4,001	4,126	3,965	4,[illegible]	[illegible]	[illegible]

	SENIOR GRADE.									
YEAR.	1886.	1887.	1888.	1889.	1890.	1891.	1892.	1893.	1894.	1895.
Boys—of the prescribed age, .	244	209	244	274	219	274	199	[illegible]	310	[illegible]
Do., Over-age, . .	[illegible]	13	7	10	11	6	7	[illegible]	[illegible]	[illegible]
Total, . . .	250	[illegible]	251	284	[illegible]	[illegible]	206	[illegible]	[illegible]	[illegible]
Girls—of the prescribed age, .	[illegible]	86	109	131	122	56	51	[illegible]	[illegible]	10[illegible]
Do., Over-age, . .	[illegible]	1	3	4	1	3	1	[illegible]	[illegible]	13
Total, . . .	98	[illegible]	113	135	123	[illegible]	[illegible]	[illegible]	10[illegible]	11[illegible]
Grand Total, . .	348	318	363	418	353	[illegible]	[illegible]	341	[illegible]	[illegible]

themselves for Examination in the years 1886, 1887, 1888, 1894, and 1895—*continued.*

Middle Grade.										
1886.	1887.	1888.	1889.	1890.	1891.	1892.	1893.	1894.	1895.	Year.
[illegible]	578	[illegible]	547	534	475	[illegible]	502	[illegible]	[illegible]	Boys—of the prescribed age.
79	[illegible]	17	[illegible]	16	34	–	78	[illegible]	[illegible]	Do., Over-age.
[illegible]	612	[illegible]	[illegible]	[illegible]	457	[illegible]	[illegible]	704	[illegible]	Total.
[illegible]	[illegible]	271	[illegible]	[illegible]	241	227	[illegible]	[illegible]	251	Girls—of the prescribed age.
18	18	[illegible]	17	6	[illegible]	–	26	[illegible]	40	Do., Over-age.
[illegible]	[illegible]	230	[illegible]	[illegible]	[illegible]	[illegible]	[illegible]	247	310	Total.
[illegible]	[illegible]	[illegible]	[illegible]	[illegible]	707	710	[illegible]	[illegible]	[illegible]	Gross Total.

Total.										
1886.	1887.	1888.	1889.	1890.	1891.	1892.	1893.	1894.	1895.	Year.
[illegible]	[illegible]	[illegible]	[illegible]	[illegible]	[illegible]	[illegible]	[illegible]	[illegible]	[illegible]	Boys—of the prescribed age.
[illegible]	127	140	[illegible]	110	125	7	342	444	[illegible]	Do., Over-age.
[illegible]	4,615	[illegible]	[illegible]	5,943	[illegible]	4,794	[illegible]	[illegible]	[illegible]	Total.
1,176	[illegible]	[illegible]	[illegible]	1,271	1,375	1,454	1,618	[illegible]	1,905	Girls—of the prescribed age.
[illegible]	19	[illegible]	[illegible]	[illegible]	[illegible]	1	91	112	181	Do., Over-age.
[illegible]	[illegible]	[illegible]	[illegible]	[illegible]	1,900	[illegible]	1,709	[illegible]	[illegible]	Total.
[illegible]	[illegible]	[illegible]	[illegible]	[illegible]	[illegible]	[illegible]	[illegible]	[illegible]	[illegible]	Gross Total.

[illegible]—Showing the Days and Hours [illegible] Examinations in the several subjects of the [illegible] were held in [illegible].

Day	[illegible]		[illegible]		[illegible]		[illegible]	
	[illegible]	[illegible]	[illegible]	[illegible]	[illegible]	Hours.	[illegible]	[illegible]
Monday, [illegible]	[illegible], ([illegible])	[illegible]	Greek, ([illegible]) Commercial—English, ([illegible]) Commercial—French, Commercial—German,	[illegible]	Greek, ([illegible]) Commercial—English, ([illegible]) Commercial—French, Commercial—German,	[illegible]	Greek, ([illegible]) Commercial—English, ([illegible]) Commercial—French, Commercial—German,	[illegible]
Tuesday, [illegible]	Drawing, [illegible],	[illegible]	Drawing, [illegible] Geometry, ([illegible]) Freehand, ([illegible]) [illegible],	[illegible]	Drawing, [illegible] Geometry, ([illegible]) Freehand, ([illegible]) [illegible],	[illegible]	Drawing, [illegible] ([illegible]) [illegible],	[illegible]
Wednesday, [illegible]	[illegible],	[illegible]	[illegible], ([illegible]) Chemistry,	[illegible]	[illegible], ([illegible]) Chemistry,	[illegible]	[illegible], ([illegible]) Chemistry,	[illegible]
Thursday, [illegible]	[illegible],	[illegible]	Italian or Spanish, ([illegible]) Shorthand,	[illegible]	Italian or Spanish, ([illegible]) Shorthand, [illegible] Writing,	[illegible]	[illegible], ([illegible]) Shorthand, [illegible] Writing,	[illegible]
Friday, [illegible]			Music,* ([illegible]) Commercial—[illegible], Botany,†	[illegible]	Music,* ([illegible]) Commercial—[illegible], Botany,†	[illegible]	Music,* ([illegible]) Commercial—[illegible], Botany,†	[illegible]

* [illegible]. † [illegible].

TABLE III.—Showing the number of Students who passed the Examination.

—	[illegible] Grade			Junior Grade			[illegible] Grade			[illegible] Grade			Total		
	Ex-amined.	Passed.	Per cent. of Passes.	Ex-amined.	Passed.	Per cent. of Passes.	Ex-amined.	Passed.	Per cent. of Passes.	Ex-amined.	Passed.	Per cent. of Passes.	Ex-amined.	Passed.	Per cent. of Passes.
[illegible] the prescribed age,	[illegible]	[illegible]	[illegible]	[illegible]	[illegible]	[illegible]	[illegible]	[illegible]	[illegible]	[illegible]	[illegible]	[illegible]	[illegible]	[illegible]	[illegible]
Do., Over age,	[illegible]	[illegible]	[illegible]	[illegible]	[illegible]	[illegible]	[illegible]	[illegible]	[illegible]	[illegible]	[illegible]	[illegible]	[illegible]	[illegible]	[illegible]
Total,	[illegible]	[illegible]	[illegible]	[illegible]	[illegible]	[illegible]	[illegible]	[illegible]	[illegible]	[illegible]	[illegible]	[illegible]	[illegible]	[illegible]	[illegible]
[illegible] the prescribed age,	[illegible]	[illegible]	[illegible]	[illegible]	[illegible]	[illegible]	[illegible]	[illegible]	[illegible]	[illegible]	[illegible]	[illegible]	[illegible]	[illegible]	[illegible]
Do., Over age,	[illegible]	[illegible]	[illegible]	[illegible]	[illegible]	[illegible]	[illegible]	[illegible]	[illegible]	[illegible]	[illegible]	[illegible]	[illegible]	[illegible]	[illegible]
Total,	[illegible]	[illegible]	[illegible]	[illegible]	[illegible]	[illegible]	[illegible]	[illegible]	[illegible]	[illegible]	[illegible]	[illegible]	[illegible]	[illegible]	[illegible]
Grand Total,	[illegible]	[illegible]	[illegible]	[illegible]	[illegible]	[illegible]	[illegible]	[illegible]	[illegible]	[illegible]	[illegible]	[illegible]	[illegible]	[illegible]	[illegible]

TABLE IV.—[illegible]

BOYS.

[illegible]	[illegible]	[illegible]	[illegible]	[illegible]	[illegible]	[illegible]	[illegible]	[illegible]	[illegible]	[illegible]	[illegible]
[illegible]	[illegible]	[illegible]	[illegible]	[illegible]	[illegible]	[illegible]	[illegible]	[illegible]	[illegible]	[illegible]	[illegible]

TABLE IV.—Showing for each subject (1) the number of students who passed with Honors, (2) the number who passed without Honors, (3) the number who failed, and (4) the total number examined; also the proportion per cent. to those examined of those who (5) passed with Honors, and (6) who passed without Honors—continued.

BOYS.

[illegible]	[illegible]
Passed with Honors,	[illegible]
" without Honors,	[illegible]
Failed,	[illegible]
Total Examined,	[illegible]
Percentage per cent. who passed with Honors,	[illegible]
Ditto, " without Honors,	[illegible]
Total Percentage passed,	[illegible]
[illegible]	
Passed with Honors,	[illegible]
" without Honors,	[illegible]
Failed,	[illegible]
Total Examined,	[illegible]
Percentage per cent. who passed with Honors,	[illegible]

TABLE IV.—Showing for each subject (1) the number of students who passed with Honours, (2) the number who passed without Honours, (3) the number who failed, and (4) the total number examined; also the proportion per cent. to those examined of those who (1) passed with Honours, and (2) who passed without Honours—continued.

BOYS.

[illegible]	[illegible]
Passed with Honours,	[illegible]
„ without Honours,	[illegible]
Failed,	[illegible]
Total Examined,	[illegible]
Percentage per cent. who passed with Honours,	[illegible]
Ditto without Honours,	[illegible]
Total Percentage passed,	[illegible]
[illegible]	[illegible]
Passed with Honours,	[illegible]
„ without Honours,	[illegible]
Failed,	[illegible]
Total Examined,	[illegible]

[illegible]	[illegible]
[illegible]	[illegible]
[illegible]	[illegible]
[illegible]	[illegible]
[illegible]	[illegible]
[illegible]	[illegible]
[illegible]	[illegible]
[illegible]	[illegible]
[illegible]	[illegible]
[illegible]	[illegible]
[illegible]	[illegible]
[illegible]	[illegible]
[illegible]	[illegible]
[illegible]	[illegible]
[illegible]	[illegible]

[illegible]														
[illegible]	[illegible]	[illegible]	[illegible]	[illegible]	[illegible]	[illegible]	[illegible]	[illegible]	[illegible]	[illegible]	[illegible]	[illegible]	[illegible]	[illegible]
[illegible]	[illegible]	[illegible]	[illegible]	[illegible]	[illegible]	[illegible]	[illegible]	[illegible]	[illegible]	[illegible]	[illegible]	[illegible]	[illegible]	[illegible]
[illegible]	[illegible]	[illegible]	[illegible]	[illegible]	[illegible]	[illegible]	[illegible]	[illegible]	[illegible]	[illegible]	[illegible]	[illegible]	[illegible]	[illegible]
[illegible]	[illegible]	[illegible]	[illegible]	[illegible]	[illegible]	[illegible]	[illegible]	[illegible]	[illegible]	[illegible]	[illegible]	[illegible]	[illegible]	[illegible]
[illegible]	[illegible]	[illegible]	[illegible]	[illegible]	[illegible]	[illegible]	[illegible]	[illegible]	[illegible]	[illegible]	[illegible]	[illegible]	[illegible]	[illegible]
[illegible]	[illegible]	[illegible]	[illegible]	[illegible]	[illegible]	[illegible]	[illegible]	[illegible]	[illegible]	[illegible]	[illegible]	[illegible]	[illegible]	[illegible]
[illegible]	[illegible]	[illegible]	[illegible]	[illegible]	[illegible]	[illegible]	[illegible]	[illegible]	[illegible]	[illegible]	[illegible]	[illegible]	[illegible]	[illegible]
[illegible]														
[illegible]	[illegible]	[illegible]	[illegible]	[illegible]	[illegible]	[illegible]	[illegible]	[illegible]	[illegible]	[illegible]	[illegible]	[illegible]	[illegible]	[illegible]
[illegible]	[illegible]	[illegible]	[illegible]	[illegible]	[illegible]	[illegible]	[illegible]	[illegible]	[illegible]	[illegible]	[illegible]	[illegible]	[illegible]	[illegible]
[illegible]	[illegible]	[illegible]	[illegible]	[illegible]	[illegible]	[illegible]	[illegible]	[illegible]	[illegible]	[illegible]	[illegible]	[illegible]	[illegible]	[illegible]
[illegible]	[illegible]	[illegible]	[illegible]	[illegible]	[illegible]	[illegible]	[illegible]	[illegible]	[illegible]	[illegible]	[illegible]	[illegible]	[illegible]	[illegible]
[illegible]	[illegible]	[illegible]	[illegible]	[illegible]	[illegible]	[illegible]	[illegible]	[illegible]	[illegible]	[illegible]	[illegible]	[illegible]	[illegible]	[illegible]
[illegible]	[illegible]	[illegible]	[illegible]	[illegible]	[illegible]	[illegible]	[illegible]	[illegible]	[illegible]	[illegible]	[illegible]	[illegible]	[illegible]	[illegible]
[illegible]	[illegible]	[illegible]	[illegible]	[illegible]	[illegible]	[illegible]	[illegible]	[illegible]	[illegible]	[illegible]	[illegible]	[illegible]	[illegible]	[illegible]

GIRLS.

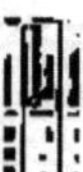

TABLE V.—Showing the number of Students to whom £50 Prize (Senior Grade), and Exhibitions were awarded.

—	Senior Grade, £50.	Middle Grade, £30 a year, tenable for two years.	Junior Grade, £20 a year, tenable for three years.	Preparatory Grade, £10 tenable for one year.	TOTAL.
Boys,	18	35	164	142	359
Girls,	7	16	59	33	115
Gross Total,	25	51	223	175	474

TABLE VI.—Showing the number of Students to whom Prizes in Books were awarded.

—	First Class Prizes.	Second Class Prizes.	Third Class Prizes.	Total.
BOYS:—				
Preparatory Grade,*	–	–	156	160
Junior "	38	47	58	118
Middle "	10	17	26	53
Senior "	7	7	30	44
Total,	55	71	272	398
GIRLS:—				
Preparatory Grade,*	–	–	42	43
Junior "	13	17	28	58
Middle "	7	8	12	27
Senior "	3	4	9	16
Total,	23	29	91	143
Gross Total,	78	100	363	541

* £1 Book Prizes, only, were awardable in the Preparatory Grade.

TABLE VII.—Showing the number of Students to whom Prizes in Composition were awarded. (Rule 51).

—	Greek.	Latin.	English.	French.	German.	Italian.	Celtic.	Spanish.	Total.
BOYS:—									
Preparatory Grade, £2, .	–	6	5	4	3	3	5	–	26
Junior „ £2, .	5	4	11	8	6	2	6	–	36
Middle „ £3, .	3	3	2	3	1	1	3	–	14
Senior „ £4, .	2	1	3	2	1	2	2	1	14
Total, . . .	10	14	21	16	8	8	12	1	90
GIRLS:—									
Preparatory Grade, £2, .	–	3	2	6	1	–	1	–	13
Junior „ £2, .	2	1	3	5	1	3	–	–	15
Middle „ £3, .	–	1	2	2	1	2	–	–	8
Senior „ £4, .	–	–	2	1	1	2	–	–	6
Total, . . .	2	5	9	14	4	7	1	–	42
Gross Total, . .	12	19	30	30	12	15	13	1	132

TABLE VIII.—Showing the number of Students to whom Special Commercial Prizes were awarded. (Rule 48.)

—	Number.	Value.
BOYS:—		£
Junior, £15, ...	5	75
Do., £10, ...	4	40
Do., £5, ...	7	35
Middle, £5, ...	1	5
Total, . . .	17	155

ACCOUNTS OF THE BOARD

(ORIGINAL ENDOWMENT).

TABLE IX.—ACCOUNTS of the BOARD (original

(A) CAPITAL

	Securities.			Cash.		
	£	s.	d.	£	s.	d.
Balance on 1st January, 1895,	1,026,841	16	6	—		
Surplus Income (from Income Account),	—			1,813	7	6
Securities purchased, viz.—Government 2¾ per cent. Stock,	1,686	18	7	—		
Cash proceeds of Securities sold,	—			—		
£	1,028,533	10	1	1,813	7	6

(B) INCOME

RECEIPTS.	£	s.	d.	£	s.	d.
In respect of the year 1894:—						
Cash Balance as per Report of 1894,	858	10	0			
Income Tax refunded,	1,015	12	6			
Results Fees refunded, 1894,	6	5	4			
Amount of cheques for Results Fees, 1894, not presented,	14	1	3			
Sale of Publications,	112	15	7			
				2,106	15	8
* [Cr. Balance, 1894, £1,987 8s. 11d.]						
In respect of the year 1895:—						
Interest of Securities,	33,240	8	6			
" on Cash on deposit,	48	12	2			
Examination Fees,	1,008	16	4			
Do. (late) Fees,	6	7	6			
Sale of Waste Paper,	3	12	10			
Restitution,	1	0	0			
Petty Expenses refunded,	0	16	4			
Sale of Publications,	181	18	1			
Refund for Cancelled Stamps,	1	11	8			
				34,585	19	6
† [Cr. Balance, 1895, £1,830 15s. 2d.]						

Endowment) for the year ended 31st December, 1895.

ACCOUNT.

	Securities. £	s.	d.	Cash. £	s.	d.
Cash invested in Government Securities (as per Contra),	—			1,813	7	6
Securities sold,	—			—		
Balance on 31st December, 1895,	1,028,588	10	1	—		
£	1,028,588	10	1	1,813	7	6

ACCOUNT.

PAYMENTS.	£	s.	d.	£	s.	d.
In respect of the year 1894:—						
Administration—						
Incidentals,	35	7	5			
Printing and Stationery,	41	18	4			
				77	5	9
Examinations—						
Printing and Stationery,	44	11	0			
Petty Expenses,	46	1	6			
Hire of Rooms,	8	10	0			
Minor Prizes,	3	0	0			
				102	2	0
In respect of the year 1895:—						
Administration—*						
Permanent Salaries,	3,104	11	0			
Writers,	501	18	5			
Rent,	64	13	4			
Printing and Stationery,	101	14	4			
Incidentals,	231	1	8			
				4,003	17	6
Examinations—*						
Examiners' Remuneration,	3,770	0	0			
Do., Locomotive Expenses,	46	10	8			
Do., Incidental and Petty Expenses,	9	1	8			
Centre Superintendents' Remuneration,	4,558	6	0			
Do., Locomotive Expenses,	528	12	7			
Do., Incidental and Petty Expenses,	558	3	4			
Hire of Rooms,	370	10	0			
Printing and Stationery,	1,836	12	8			
Petty Expenses,	448	10	6			
Locomotive do.,	5	5	6			
				12,132	14	6

[illegible]

	[illegible]	[illegible]		[illegible]	[illegible]
	£ s. d.	£ s. d.		£ s. d.	£ s. d.
[illegible]	[illegible]	—	[illegible]	[illegible]	[illegible]
[illegible]	—	[illegible]	[illegible]	[illegible]	—
£	[illegible]	[illegible]	£	[illegible]	[illegible]

[illegible]

	£ s. d.			£ s. d.
[illegible]	[illegible]	[illegible]		[illegible]
[illegible]	[illegible]	[illegible]		[illegible]
[illegible]	[illegible]	[illegible]	[illegible]	
[illegible]	[illegible]	[illegible]	[illegible]	
[illegible]	[illegible]			[illegible]
[illegible]	[illegible]			
[illegible]	[illegible]			
[illegible]	[illegible]			

TABLE XI.—THE "BURKE MEMORIAL FUND."

ACCOUNT FOR THE YEAR ENDED 31ST DECEMBER, 18[illegible].

CAPITAL ACCOUNT.

Government 2¾ per cent. Consols,	£[illegible]	Balance at Dec. 31, 18[illegible], . .	£[illegible]

INCOME ACCOUNT.

	£	s.	d.		£	s.	d.
Balance on 1st January, 18[illegible], ...	[illegible]	[illegible]	[illegible]	Prizes (vide page [illegible]), ...	[illegible]	[illegible]	[illegible]
5 Jan., Quarter's Dividend on 2¾ per cent. Consols,	[illegible]	[illegible]	[illegible]	Printing and Stationery, ...	[illegible]	[illegible]	[illegible]
5 April, „ „ „ „ „	[illegible]	[illegible]	[illegible]	Balance at Dec. 31, 18[illegible], ...	[illegible]	[illegible]	[illegible]
5 July, „ „ „ „ „	[illegible]	[illegible]	[illegible]				
5 Oct., „ „ „ „ „	[illegible]	[illegible]	[illegible]				
	£[illegible]	[illegible]	[illegible]		£[illegible]	[illegible]	[illegible]

Given under our Common Seal

this 20th day of March, 1890.

Present at Board Meeting when Seal was affixed,

T. J. BELLINGHAM BRADY,
JOHN C. MALET, } *Assistant Commissioners*

NAMES OF THE COMMISSIONERS

OF

INTERMEDIATE EDUCATION (IRELAND).

Right Hon. J. T. BALL, LL.D., D.C.L., Chairman.

Right Hon. C. PALLES, LL.D., Lord Chief Baron of the Exchequer in Ireland, Vice-Chairman.

Rev. GEORGE SALMON, D.D., D.C.L., LL.D., F.R.S., Provost, Trinity College, Dublin.

The Right Hon. O'CONOR DON, D.L., LL.D.

Rev. W. TODD MARTIN, D.D., D.LIT.

DAVID G. BARKLEY, Esq., LL.D.

His Grace The Most Rev. WILLIAM J. WALSH, D.D., Archbishop of Dublin.

ASSISTANT COMMISSIONERS.

T. J. BELLINGHAM BRADY, LL.D.

JOHN C. MALET, M.A., F.R.S.

APPENDIX I.

LIST of PERSONS from whom the Examiners for 1895 were selected, with the approval of the LORD LIEUTENANT (Rule 6).

GREEK AND LATIN.

Armour, Rev. James B., M.A. (R.U.I.)
Barrett, Rev. R.
Beare, John I., M.A., F.T.C.D.
Bryce, A. Hamilton, LL.D.
Bury, John B., M.A. (Dub.), F.T.C.D.
Butler, Rev. M. J., B.A., D.D.
Conan, Arthur, M.A. (R.U.I.), B.A. (Dub.), Sen. Mod., T.C.D.
Cotter, W. E. P., B.A., 1st Sen. Mod., T.C.D.
Crowe, Rev. Jeremiah, St. Patrick's College, Thurles.
Dickie, John, B.A. (Dub.), 1st Sen. Mod., T.C.D.
Dougan, T. W., M.A., Ex-Fellow, St. John's College, Cambridge, Professor of Latin, Queen's College, Belfast.
Dowdall, Rev. Launcelot D., LL.B. (Dub.), M.A. (Oxon.), 1st Sen. Mod., T.C.D., University Student.
Doyle, Charles F., M.A. (F.R.U.I.), B.A. (Dub.), Sen. Mod., T.C.D.
Doyle, Robert, B.A. (Dub.), Moderator, T.C.D.
Hamilton, A. B., M.A., LL.B. (R.U.I.)
Hayes, Rev. Laurence J., D.D., Professor, St. Patrick's College, Thurles.
Healy, John, B.A.
Hitchcock, Francis R. M., B.A., Dub., 1st Sen. Mod., Univ. Student, T.C.D.
Keene, Charles, M.A. (Dub.), Sen. Mod., T.C.D.
Kelly, Very Rev. J. J., Canon.
Kennedy, Wm., M.A., Univ. Student, R.U.I., B.A. (Dub.), Sen. Mod., T.C.D.
Kerin, R. C. R., B.A., 1st Class Classical Honours, London.
Maguire, Rev. E., Professor of Classics, St. Patrick's College, Maynooth.
Mannix, Rev. D., Professor, St. Patrick's College, Maynooth.
M'Glone, Rev. Peter, D.D.
M'Neill, Hugh A., B.A., R.U.I.
M'Rory, Rev. Joseph, D.D., Professor, St. Patrick's College, Maynooth.
Molahan, John P., M.A. (Dub.), Sen. Mod., T.C.D.
Montgomery, Robert, M.A., University Student (R.U.I.), B.A., 1st Class Classical Tripos, Cantab.
Montgomrey, Malcolm, M.A. (Dub.), 1st Sen. Mod., T.C.D., Univ. Student.
Morgan, Rev. W. Moore, M.A., T.C.D.
Newsome, Clarence, M.A. (R.U.I.), Sen. Mod., T.C.D.
O'Dea, Henry, B.A. (Dub.), Mod., T.C.D., M.A., R.U.I.
O'Farrell, Very Rev. J., Canon.
O'Neill, Rev. James.
Palmer, Arthur, M.A. (Dub.), F.T.C.D., Prof. of Latin, Univ. of Dublin.
Patton, Rev. Samuel, M.A.
Purser, Louis C., D.LITT., F.T.C.D.
Rice, Rev. James, B.D. (Dub.), Sen. Mod., T.C.D.
Ridgeway, William, M.A. (Dub.), Ex-Professor of Greek, Queen's College, Cork; Fellow, Gonville and Caius College, Disney Professor of Archæology, Cambridge.
Roberts, Theodore M., M.A. (Dub.)

Rowan, William H., M.A., Univ. Student (R.U.I.)
Rutherford, H. E., B.A., LL.B.
Ryan, Rev. Innocent, Professor, St. Patrick's College, Thurles.
Sandford, Philip George, M.A. (Dub.), Professor of Latin, Queen's College, Galway.
Starkie, W. J. M., M.A., F.T.C.D.
Thompson, D'Arcy W., M.A. (Cantab.), F.R.U.I., Professor of Greek, Queen's College, Galway.
Tyrrell, Robert Y., M.A., D.LITT. (Dub.), F.T.C.D., Professor of Greek, University of Dublin.
Wilkins, Rev. George, M.A. (Dub.), F.T.C.D.
Wilson, Herbert, B.A. (Dub.), 1st Sen. Mod., T.C.D.

ENGLISH.

Allen, Henry J., B.A. (Dub.), 1st Sen. Mod., T.C.D.
Bailey, William F., B.A. (Dub.), 1st Sen. Mod., T.C.D.
Barlow, Jane.
Barry, Rev. Louis Aug., LL.D. (Dub.), 1st Sen. Mod., T.C.D.
Bastable, C. F., B.A. (Dub.), Prof. of Political Economy, Univ. of Dublin.
Boyd, Andrew, M.A. (R.U.I.)
Brown, Samuel Lombard, B.A. (R.U.I.)
Carmichael, Rev. Frederick F., LL.D. (Dub.)
Cherry, Richard R., M.A., LL.D. (Dub.), Reid Professor of Constitutional and Criminal Law, T.C.D.
Clancy, Rev. John J., D.D., Professor of English Literature, St. Patrick's College, Maynooth.
Coghlan, Rev. Daniel, St. Patrick's College, Maynooth.
Colclough, John D.
Cooke, John, B.A. (Dub.), Professor, Church of Ireland Training College, Kildare-place.
Coyne, William P., M.A. (R.U.I.)
Croly, D., M.A. (R.U.I.), Professor of English Literature, Catholic Training College, Drumcondra.
Cusack, John.
Dixon, G. Y., B.A., T.C.D.
Dixon, W. M., B.A., LL.B., 1st Sen. Mod., T.C.D.
Donnellan, Rev. James, St. Patrick's College, Maynooth.
Donovan, R., B.A. (R.U.I.)
Evans, Rev. Henry, D.D.
Fetherstonhaugh, Godfrey, B.A. (Dub.), 1st Sen. Mod., T.C.D., Univ. Student.
Fitzgibbon, Henry M., M.A. (Dub.), Senior Mod., T.C.D.
Fitz-Henry, William A., M.A., LL.B.
Fogarty, Rev. M., St. Patrick's College, Maynooth.
Gilliland, W. L., B.A., LL.B. (Dub.), Senior Mod., T.C.D.
Graham, Wm., M.A. (Dub.), Professor of Jurisprudence and Political Economy, Queen's College, Belfast.
Hardy, William J., LL.D. (Dub.), Sen. Mod., T.C.D.
Harrison, Thomas, B.A., LL.B. (R.U.I.)
Henry, Rev. J. Elgar, M.A. (R.U.I.)
Herdman, John C., M.A., Sen. Mod., T.C.D.
Humphreys, John, B.A.
Hyde, Douglas, LL.D.
Joyce, P. W., LL.D., Ex-Professor, Board of National Education.
Keane, A. H., B.A.
Kehoe, Daniel, B.A. (Dub.), Senior Mod., T.C.D.

Lennox, P. J., B.A. (R.U.I.)
Lyster, Mary A., M.A.
Lyster, Thomas W., B.A. (Dub.), 1st Senior Mod., T.C.D., Assistant Librarian, National Library of Ireland.
M'Bride, Rev. J. B., B.A. (R.U.I.)
M'Donald, Rev. Walter, St. Patrick's College, Maynooth.
Magennis, William, M.A. (F.R.U.I.)
MacMullan, S. J., M.A. (R.U.I.), Professor of History and English Literature, Queen's College, Belfast.
Macran, Rev. Frederick W., B.A. (Dub.), 1st Sen. Mod., T.C.D.
Macran, Henry S., M.A., F.T.C.D.
Magaw, R. D., M.A., LL.B. (R.U.I.)
Murphy, James.
Murphy, Katharine, M.A., University Student (R.U.I.)
Nash, Rev. Francis L., M.A. (Oxon.)
Newcombe, Rev. J. D. R., B.A., B.D. (Dub.), Sen. Mod., T.C.D.
Nicolls, Archibald J., LL.B. (Dub.)
O'Leary, Rev. Patrick, St. Patrick's College, Maynooth.
O'Loan, Rev. Daniel, St. Patrick's College, Maynooth.
Osborne, R. E., M.A.
Park, John, M.A. D.LITT. (R.U.I.), F.R.U.I., Professor of Logic and Metaphysics, Queen's College, Belfast.
Rea, Rev. George T., M.A.
Redmond, Frederick, B.A. (Dub.), Sen. Mod., T.C.D.
Rolleston, T. W., B.A., T.C.D.
Rowley, James, M.A., Professor of Modern History and English Literature, Univ. College, Bristol.
Savage-Armstrong, George F., M.A. (Dub.), F.R.U.I.; Professor of History and English Literature, Queen's College, Cork.
Scratton, Thomas, B.A. (Oxon.)
Semple, R. J., M.A., University Student (R.U.I.)
Smyth, Rev. J. Paterson, B.A., LL.B. (Dub.), Sen. Mod., T.C.D.
Stanton, Lucy Vere.
Steele, L. Edward, B.A. (Dub.), Professor in the Church of Ireland Training College, Kildare-place.
Story, Mary, M.A., University Student, R.U.I.
Taylor, John F., B.A.
Walland, Rev. Charles W., B.A. (Dub.), Sen. Mod., T.C.D.
Whelan, Rev. Denis, St. John's College, Waterford.
Whitty, R. C. J., B.A. (Dub.), Sen. Mod., T.C.D.
Willson, Rev. Thomas B., M.A. (Dub.), 1st Sen. Mod., T.C.D.
Witherow, Rev. J. M., M.A. (R.U.I.)
Wright, A. E., B.A. (Dub.), 1st Senior Mod., T.C.D.

French.

Amours, F. J., B. ès L. French Master, Glasgow Academy.
Bacon, John W., M.A. (R.U.I.)
Barbier, Paul E. E., Lecturer, French Language and Literature, Univ. Coll., South Wales, Cardiff.
Barbier, Georges E., Lecturer in French, The Athenæum, Glasgow.
Barrère, A., Prof. of French, Royal Military Academy, Woolwich.
Boielle, James, B.A. (Paris).
Bue, Henry, B. ès L. (Univ. Gall.)
Butler, W. F., M.A., University Student (R.U.I.)

Cogery, A., B.A., L.L. (Paris), Examiner in French, Trinity Coll., London.
D'Auquier, Rev. E. C., M.A. (Cantab.)
D'Auquier, T. C.
Desnoduu, Lydia.
Dupuis, Alexandre L., B.A.
Egerton, Charles W., M.A. (Dub.), Senior Mod., T.C.D.
Hogan, Rev. J. F., St. Patrick's Coll., Maynooth.
Janau, Elphege, Assistant Examiner in the University of London.
Ludwig, A., B.A. (Univ. Gallic).
M'Weeney, Edmond J., M.A. (R.U.I.)
Masséd, J. F. P.
Miget, N., B. es L.
Nil, Otto C., M.A., London.
Nolan, Pierce L., B.A.
Oger, V., French Lecturer, Univ. Coll., Liverpool.
Spencer, Frederic, M.A., PH.D., Professor of Modern Languages, University College, Bangor.
Voegelin, A., B.A. (London).

GERMAN.

Buchheim, C. A., PH.D., Prof. of German in King's College, London.
Fischer, E. L.
Hager, Herman, PH.D.
Heinemann, N., Prof. of German, Crystal Palace School of Arts & Sciences.
Hennig, Curt, M.A.
Houston, Rev. J. D. C., B.A.
Lange, Franz, PH.D., Prof. of German, Royal Mil. Academy, Woolwich.
Meissner, A. L., PH.D., Prof. Modern Languages, Queen's Coll., Belfast.
Oswald, E., M.A., PH.D. (Goettingen), Instructor in German to the Royal Naval College, Greenwich.
Schlomka, C., M.A., PH.D.
Selss, Albert M., M.A., LL.D. (Dub.), Sen. Mod., T.C.D., PH.D., Professor of German, University of Dublin.
Steinberger, Valentine, M.A. (R.U.I.), Professor of Modern Languages, Queen's College, Galway.

ITALIAN.

Farinelli, A., Professor of Italian, University College, London.
Marosini, Francesca.
Murphy, Rev. W. H., D.D.
O'Keeffe, Rev. Barth. A., D.D.
Ricci, Luigi, Prof. City of London College.

SPANISH.

Steinberger, Valentine, M.A., R.U.I., Professor of Modern Languages, Queen's College, Galway.

CELTIC.

Connolly, William P., B.A.
Flannery, T.
Hogan, Rev. Edmund, S.J.
McCarthy, Rev. B., D.D.
Molloy, John, B. es L.

Murphy, Rev. James E. H., B.A. (Dub.), Ex-Siz., Bedell Sch., T.C.D.
O'Duffy, Richard J., Hon. Sec., Society for the Preservation of the Irish Language.
O'Growney, Rev. Eugene, Professor, St. Patrick's College, Maynooth.
Olden, Rev. Thomas, B.A.

MATHEMATICS.

Alexander, J. J., M.A., (R.U.I.), B.A. (Cantab.)
Allman, George J., M.A., LL.D., F.R.S., Ex-Professor of Mathematics, Queen's College, Galway.
Anglin, A. H., M.A. (R.U.I.), B.A. (Cantab.), F.R.S.E., Professor of Mathematics, Queen's College, Cork.
Barrett, Rev. Michael.
Bergin, William, M.A. (Dub.), Sen. Mod., T.C.D.
Bernard, Rev. J. H., M.A., B.D. (Dub.), F.T.C.D.
Browne, J. J.
Burnside, Wm. S., M.A. D.SC. (Dub.), F.T.C.D., Prof. of Mathematics, Univ. of Dublin.
Carroll, Rev. P. J.
Coates, W. M., M.A. (Dub.), B.A. (Cantab.), Sen. Mod., T.C.D., Fellow of Queen's College, Cambridge.
Culverwell, Edward P., M.A., F.T.C.D.
Dawson, H. G., B.A. (Dub.), 1st Sen. Mod., T.C.D., M.A. (Cantab.), Fellow of Christ's College, Cambridge.
Dickey, Rev. R. H. F., M.A., B.D.
Dowling, E. Hughes, B.A. (R.U.I.), Math. Tutor, University College, Stephen's-green, Dublin.
England, John, M.A. (Dub.), Professor of Natural Philosophy, Queen's College, Cork.
Fry, M. W. Joseph, M.A. (Dub.), F.T.C.D.
Gibney, James J., M.A., University Student (R.U.I.)
Graham, Christopher, M.A. (Dub. and Cantab.), 1st Sen. Mod., T.C.D., Ex-Fellow, Gonville and Caius College, Cambridge.
Griffin, Gerald.
Griffin, Robert W., LL.D. (Dub.)
Inwood, Thos. W., B.A., Professor of Mathematics, St. Gregory's College, Downside, Bath.
Johnston, J. P., M.A. (Dub.), Sen. Mod., T.C.D.
Johnston, Swift P., M.A. (Dub.), 1st Sen. Mod., T.C.D., Univ. Student.
Joly, C. J., M.A., F.T.C.D.
Kelly, Patrick.
Larmor, Joseph, M.A. (R.U.I.), M.A. (Cantab.), Senior Wrangler, Fellow of St. John's College, Cambridge, F.R.S.
Leebody, John R., D.SC. (R.U.I.), Professor of Mathematics and Natural Philosophy, Magee College, Londonderry.
Lennon, Rev. Francis, D.D., Professor of Mathematics and Natural Philosophy, St. Patrick's College, Maynooth.
Lyster, Arthur E., M.A. (Dub.), Sen. Mod., T.C.D., Assistant Astronomer, Dunsink Observatory.
M'Weeney, Henry C., M.A. (F.R.U.I.), Sen. Mod. (T.C.D.)
Minchin, George M., M.A. (Dub.), Professor of Applied Mathematics, Royal Indian Engineering College, Cooper's Hill.
Moran, Rev. Francis, M.A. (DUB.)
O'Dea, Rev. Thomas, Professor, St. Patrick's College, Maynooth.

Orr, Wm. M'F., M.A. (R.U.I.), Sen. Wrangler, Fellow of St. John's College, Cambridge; Prof. of Applied Mathematics and Mechanism, Royal College of Science, Ireland.
O'Sullivan, A. C., B.A. (Dub.), F.T.C.D.
Panton, Arthur W., M.A., D.SC. (Dub.), F.T.C.D.
Power, Rev. Thos. E., Prof. of Mathematics, St. Patrick's Coll., Thurles.
Rambaut, Arthur A., M.A., D.SC., Astronomer Royal of Ireland.
Rea, James C., B.A. (R.U.I.), Professor in the Church of Ireland Training College, Kildare-place.
Roberts, W. R. Westropp, M.A. (Dub.), F.T.C.D.
Russell, R., M.A. (Dub.), F.T.C.D.
Smith, Charles, M.A. (R.U.I.), M.A. (Dub.), 1st Sen. Mod. (T.C.D.), Univ. Student.
Tarleton, Francis A., LL.D. (Dub.), F.T.C.D.
Warren, Rev. Isaac, M.A.
Yates, James, B.A., Sen. Mod., T.C.D.

Arithmetic and Book-keeping.

Dowd, Rev. James, B.A. (Dub.), Sen. Mod., T.C.D.
Bond, H. S., Royal Bank of Ireland.
Dowling, P. A. E., B.A. (R.U.I.)
Ellis, Wm. R., M.A., LL.B. (Dub.), Local Gov. Auditor, Ireland.
Farrelly, Daniel.
Fitzpatrick, S., Prof. of Mathematics, Catholic Training Coll., Drumcondra.
Hughes, Rev. William, D.D. (Dub.)
Irwin, Rev. Charles K., D.D., (Dub.)
Keoghan, Rev. Patrick, B.A. (R.U.I.)
Macbeth, Rev. John, LL.D. (Dub.)
O'Brien, Edward T., Accountant, Mining Co. of Ireland.
O'Connor, George E., B.A.
Sutcliffe, Rev. Thomas, B.A. (Dub.)
Tristram, Rev. John W., M.A. (Dub.), Sen. Mod., T.C.D., Diocesan Inspector and Secretary, Diocesan Board of Education.
Warnock, Rev. W. J., B.A. (R.U.I.)
Whitton, Frederick A., Accountant, Representative Church Body.

Natural Philosophy.

Anderson, Alexander, M.A., Fellow of Sydney Sussex College, Cambridge, Professor of Nat. Phil., Queen's College, Galway.
Barrett, W. F., F.R.S.E., Professor of Physics, R.C.SC.I.
Brown, Wm., Demonstrator in Physics, Royal Coll. of Science, Dublin.
Coffey, George, B.E. (Dub.), Sen. Mod., T.C.D.
Doherty, J. J., LL.D. (Dub.), Sen. Mod., T.C.D.
Fitzgerald, George F., M.A. (Dub.), F.R.S., F.T.C.D.
Johnston, Margaret E., B.A.
Joly, John, D.SC., F.R.S.
Larmor, Alex., M.A. (R.U.I.), B.A. (Cantab.), Fellow of Clare College, Cambridge.
Moore, Hugh Kerr, B.A. (Dub.), 1st Sen. Mod., T.C.D.
Oram, John E., M.B. (R.U.I.), M.A., Ex-Professor of Mathematics, &c., Univ. of Windsor, N.S.
Paul, John, B.A. (R.U.I.)
Preston, Thomas, M.A. (Dub.), F.R.U.I., Sen. Mod., T.C.D.

Scott, A. W., M.A. (Dub.), Professor of Physical Science, St. David's College, Lampeter, South Wales.
Stewart, John Huston, B.A., F.R.U.I., B.SC. (London); Professor of Experimental Physics, University College, Dublin.

CHEMISTRY.

Adeney, Walter E., F.I.C., A.R.C.SC.I.
Bell, Chichester, M.B. (Dub.), Sen. Mod., T.C.D.
Campbell, John, M.B. (Dub.), F.R.U.I., Professor, University Coll., Dub.
Davy, Edmund W., M.A., M.D. (Dub.)
Dixon, Augustus E., M.D., F.C.S., Prof. of Chemistry, Queen's Coll., Cork.
Falkiner, Ninian M., M.B., M.CH. (Dub.), F.C.S.I.
Lapper, Edwin, L.K.Q.C.P.I., Lec. in Chem., Ledwich School of Medicine.
Letts, Edmund A., PH.D., F.C.S., Prof. of Chemistry, Queen's Coll., Belfast.
Macmillan, John, Laboratory, Royal College of Surgeons, Ireland.
M'Hugh, Michael, M.B. (Dub.), Senior Mod., T.C.D.
Moss, Richard J., F.C.S., F.I.C., Registrar and Chemical Analyst, Royal Dublin Society.
Pratt, J. Dallas, M.A., M.D.
Reynolds, James Emerson, M.D. (Dub.), F.R.S., Professor of Chemistry, University of Dublin.
Robertson, Mary W., M.A. (R.U.I.)
Werner, Emil A., F.C.S.

BOTANY.

Anderson, R. J., M.A., M.D. (R.U.I.), Prof. of Nat. Hist., Queen's Coll., Galway.
Boulger, G. S., F.L.S., F.G.S.
Dixon, Henry H., B.A., Sen. Mod., T.C.D.
Hanna, William, M.A.
Hartog, Marcus M., M.A., D.SC., F.L.S., F.R.U.I., Prof. Nat. Hist., Queen's College, Cork.
Melville, Alex. G., M.D. (Edin.), M.R.C.S.E., Ex-Professor of Natural History, Queen's College, Galway.
Pim, Greenwood, M.A. (Dub.), Sen. Mod., T.C.D.
Sigerson, George, M.D., M.CH. (R.U.I.)
Wilson, Andrew, PH.D., F.R.S.E., F.L.S.
Wright, Ed. Perceval, M.D. (Dub.), Professor of Botany, University of Dublin.

DRAWING.

Atkinson, George M., Exam., Science and Art Dept., South Kensington.
Bowler, H. A., Inspector and Assist. Director, Art Division, Science and Art Department, South Kensington.
Carroll, John, Art Master, Hammersmith Training Coll.
Conan, Florence.
Craister, Walter, Head Master, Government School of Art, Stevenson Memorial Hall, Chesterfield.
Crowther, W. E.
Harris, Robert, Art Master, St. Paul's School, London.
Jackson, Joshua, Art Master, Manchester Grammar School.
Keogh, Alice M.
Langman, A. W. F., Senior Drawing Inspector to the London School Board.

Lindsay, Thomas M., Drawing Master, Rugby School.
O'Brien, Edward Stewart, B.A., B.E. (R.U.I.)
Prendergast, P. J., B.E.
Rawle, John S., F.S.A.
Scully, T., B.E. (R.U.I.)
Vinter, J. A., London.

THEORY OF MUSIC.

Allison, H., MUS.D. (Dub.)
Bewerunge, Rev. H.
Elliott, Stanislaus.
Garrett, George, MUS.D., M.A. (Cantab.)
Gater, William H., B.A., MUS.D. (Dub.)
Glok, Thomas, MUS.D. (Dub.)
Goodwin, W. G.
Hanratty, J. H.
Hoffmann, F.
Houghton, Edward.
Joze, T. R. G., MUS.D. (Dub.)
Kerbusch, L., MUS.D. (Dub.)
Malone, Robert, MUS.D. (Dub.)
Marks, J. Chr., MUS.D. (Oxon.)
Marks, T. Osborne, MUS.D.
Muntz, Ellie.
Rogers, Brendan J.
Seymour, Joseph, MUS.B.
Smith, Joseph, MUS.D. (Dub.)
Taylor, Charlotte M., MUS.B. (R.U.I.)

DOMESTIC ECONOMY.

Barrington-Ward, M. J., M.A. (Oxon.), H.M. Inspector of Schools.
Gallaher, Fannie H.
Harrison, W. Jerome, Science Demonstrator, Birmingham School Board, &c.
McCarthy, Margaret.
Moore, Louisa.
Todd, Mary Bellingham.

SHORTHAND.

Boyle, M. F.
Bunbury, George William.
Healy, F. C. Wallis.
Holt, Henry.
Hunt, Henry.
Ryan, Charles.

APPENDIX II.

LIST OF EXAMINERS

SELECTED, WITH THE APPROVAL OF THE LORD LIEUTENANT, TO CONDUCT THE EXAMINATIONS IN 1895.

GREEK AND LATIN.

Armour, Rev. James B., M.A. (R.U.I.)
Crowe, Rev. Jeremiah, St. Patrick's College, Thurles.
Dougan, T. W., M.A., Ex-Fellow, St. John's College, Cambridge, Professor of Latin, Queen's College, Belfast.
Keene, Charles, M.A. (Dub.), Professor of Greek, Queen's College, Cork.
Kelly, Very Rev. J. J., Canon.
Kerin, R. C. B., B.A. (London).
Mannix, Rev. D., Professor, St. Patrick's College, Maynooth.
Purser, Louis C., D. LITT., F.T.C.D.
Rice, Rev. James, D.D. (Dub.)
Ryan, Rev. Innocent, Professor, St. Patrick's College, Thurles.
Wilkins, Rev. George, M.A. (Dub.), F.T.C.D.

ENGLISH.

Barry, Rev. Louis Aug., LL.D. (Dub.)
Bastable, C. F., LL.D. (Dub.), Professor of Political Economy, University of Dublin.
Cooke, John, B.A. (Dub.), Professor, Church of Ireland Training College, Kildare-place.
Croly, D., M.A. (R.U.I.), Professor of English Literature, Catholic Training College, Drumcondra.
Donovan, R., B.A. (R.U.I.)
Evans, Rev. Henry, D.D.
Henry, Rev. J. Edgar, M.A. (R.U.I.)
Joyce, P. W., LL.D., Ex-Professor, Board of National Education.
M'Bride, Rev. J. R., B.A. (R.U.I.)
Macran, Henry S., M.A., F.T.C.D.
Magennis, William, M.A., F.R.U.I.
Murphy, Katharine, B.A.
O'Leary, Rev. Patrick, St. Patrick's College, Maynooth.
O'Loan, Rev. Daniel, St. Patrick's College, Maynooth.
Scrutton, Thomas, B.A. (Oxon.)
Semple, R. J., M.A., University Student (R.U.I.)
Smyth, Rev. J. Paterson, B.A., LL.D. (Dub.), Sen. Mod., T.C.D.

FRENCH.

Amours, F. J., B. ès L., French Master, Glasgow Academy.
Barbier, Georges E., Lecturer in French, The Athenæum, Glasgow.

Barrère, A., Professor of French, Royal Military Academy, Woolwich.
Boiello, James, B.L. (Paris).
Cogery, A., B.A., L.L. (Paris), Examiner in French, Trinity College, London.
Decondun, Lydie.
Hogan, Rev. J. F., St. Patrick's College, Maynooth.
Janau, Elphege, Assistant Examiner in the University of London.

German.

Selss, Albert M., M.A., LL.D. (Dub.), Sen. Mod., T.C.D., PH.D., Professor of German, University of Dublin.

Spanish.

Steinberger, Valentine, M.A. (R.U.I.), Professor of Modern Languages, Queen's College, Galway.

Italian.

Murphy, Rev. W. H., D.D.

Celtic.

Flannery, T. J.

Mathematics.

Alexander, J. J., M.A. (R.U.I.), B.A. (Cantab.)
Barrett, Rev. Michael.
Dowling, E. Hughes, M.A. (R.U.I.), Math. Tutor, University College, Stephen's-green, Dublin.
England, John, M.A. (Dub.), Professor of Natural Philosophy, Queen's College, Cork.
Gibney, James J., M.A., F.R.U.I.
Inwood, Thomas W., B.A., Professor of Mathematics, St. Gregory's College, Downside, Bath.
Leebody, John R., D.SC. (R.U.I.), Professor of Mathematics and Natural Philosophy, Magee College, Londonderry.
Lennon, Rev. Francis, D.D., Professor of Mathematics and Natural Philosophy, St. Patrick's College, Maynooth.
Lyster, Arthur E., M.A. (Dub.), Sen. Mod., T.C.D., Assistant Astronomer, Dunsink Observatory.
Orr, Wm. M'F., M.A. (R.U.I.), Sen. Wrangler, Fellow of St. John's College, Cambridge; Professor of Applied Mathematics and Mechanism, Royal College of Science, Ireland.
Panton, Arthur W., M.A., D.SC. (Dub.), F.T.C.D.
Rea, James C., B.A. (R.U.I.), Professor in the Church of Ireland Training College, Kildare-place.
Smith, Charles, M.A. (R.U.I.), M.A. (Dub.), 1st Sen. Mod., T.C.D., University Student.

Arithmetic and Book-keeping.

Fitzpatrick, S., Professor of Mathematics, Catholic Training College, Drumcondra.
Hughes, Rev. William, D.D. (Dub.)
Irwin, Ven. Chas. K., D.D. (Dub.)
O'Brien, Edward T., Accountant, Mining Co. of Ireland.
O'Connor, George R., B.A.

NATURAL PHILOSOPHY.

Coffey, George, B.E. (Dub.)
Joly, John, D.SC., F.R.S.

CHEMISTRY.

Moss, Richard J., F.C.S., F.I.C., Registrar and Chemical Analyst, Royal Dublin Society.

BOTANY.

Dixon, Henry H., B.A., Sen. Mod., T.C.D.

DRAWING.

Carroll, John, Art Master, Hammersmith Training College.
Keogh, Alice M.
Lindsay, Thomas M., Drawing Master, Rugby School.
O'Brian, Edward Stewart, B.A., B.E. (R.U.I.)

THEORY OF MUSIC.

Gick, Thomas, MUS.D. (Dub.)

DOMESTIC ECONOMY.

Moore, Louisa.
Todd, Mary Bellingham.

SHORTHAND.

Boyle, M. F.
Bunbury, George William.

APPENDIX III.

EXTRACTS FROM THE REPORTS OF THE EXAMINERS, 1895.

GREEK.

SENIOR GRADE.—FIRST PAPER.

Report of Rev. GEORGE WILKINS, M.A.

On the whole the answering of the candidates in this Grade was disappointing. The parsing of verbs and the answers to questions in Syntax were often incorrect. The majority of the candidates had no idea of continuous composition, though a few composed well. In translation they did considerably better, but in many cases a "crib" had been learned by rote. The girls, who are but few, did creditably.

MIDDLE GRADE.—FIRST PAPER.

Report of Rev. GEORGE WILKINS, M.A.

The grammar questions were well answered. The composition was fairly, and in many cases excellently, done. Better still was the rendering of the scenes from Medea. The girls did passably, but were few in number. The paper set was evidently not above the heads of the candidates, nor did the answers to the questions involve an overwhelming amount of writing.

JUNIOR GRADE.—FIRST PAPER.—BOYS AND GIRLS.

Report of Rev. JAMES RICE, B.D.

This being the first time I have examined in Greek for the Board, I cannot make a comparison between the answering in this and previous years. I can, however, say that in very many cases the answering was remarkably good, between thirty and forty boys, I think, if not more having obtained upwards of ninety-three per cent., while the general answering was, on the whole, very satisfactory. The Grammar, with the exception of question 5 (requiring the plural number of certain parts of Greek verbs of common occurrence), was well done by nearly all the serious candidates, and the translation of the Greek was very good. The writing of many good papers was not as careful as it should be, and candidates should try to secure that the Examiner can make out what they intend to write, especially in Greek words.

With regard to the answering of the girls on this paper, having never examined papers in Greek from girls before, I was quite surprised to find it of such a high order. Out of the fifteen papers examined, the composition was very good in more than half, and fair in most of all the others. The Grammar questions were well answered in almost every paper, and the neatness of the work was particularly observable.

Preparatory Grade.—First Paper—Boys and Girls.

Report of Rev. George Wilkins, M.A.

The answering in this Grade was on the whole good. In composition, as might be expected, the candidates were not very strong, though some acquitted themselves admirably. The paper set was meant to be level with the powers of the students, and not discouraging to them, for it is very plain to an Examiner that boys find the Greek Grammar no easy task to master. The few girls who presented themselves were better prepared than last year.

Senior Grade.—Second Paper.—Boys and Girls.

Report of Thomas W. Dougan, M.A.

I have examined the Second Paper in Greek of the Senior Grade.

I find the results this year very similar to those which I observed last year. The candidates seemed in earnest in their work, and had not, as a rule, neglected any part of the Examination.

Decidedly weak papers were rare. An intimate and sound acquaintance with the first book of the Iliad was very usually displayed.

The work upon the metre was still rather disappointing. Most candidates knew the rules of the metre, but very few could specify the position of the *main* caesura correctly in all the three lines set before them.

The verse passage for unseen translation was better done by most candidates than the prose passage, though both were taken from unprescribed portions of the prescribed authors. The fact is that the bulk of the candidates have evidently not got into the swing of the Demosthenic period. This, it seems to me, they may effect by reading over from time to time, at the same rate of speed as they would read a piece of English prose, a few pages of their prescribed speech of Demosthenes with which they have previously become well acquainted.

A few of the candidates sent in work which was very satisfactory from beginning to end, and such that if they work in a similar spirit at a University I should expect them to attain to high distinction there.

Middle Grade.—Second Paper.—Boys and Girls.

Report of Thomas W. Dougan, M.A.

I have examined these candidates in Xenophon, unseen translation, and Greek History.

I found much good work, but it seemed to me that many of the candidates had not done their best. There seemed to be a certain flippancy and lack of seriousness, of which I found few traces among the candidates of the Preparatory and Senior Grades. I inferred this from the fact that it was not uncommon to find part of the work done well, and the rest omitted or run through in a very different spirit In many cases the first questions (on the prescribed author) were so well done that I expected to find the candidate securing a high total, but as I proceeded I found that he had neglected the unseen translation, or the history, or both of those subjects. Others again answered the history questions or did the unseen extracts, but let the prescribed author alone. Quite a number who gained only about forty per cent. upon the paper, seemed fit to have taken very high marks if they had gone steadily through the paper in the style in which the best part of their work was done.

JUNIOR GRADE.—SECOND PAPER.—BOYS AND GIRLS.

Report of R. C. R. KEENE, B.A.

On the whole the answering was very satisfactory. There were, of course, several papers which showed little or no knowledge of Greek; but, on the other hand, there were several papers of high excellence. A satisfactory feature of the examination was the rendering of the unseen passage. The excellence of the translation in several cases showed that the students had not crammed their Greek but understood their work. The prescribed author was known by most. I should like, however, to point out an error into which several boys fall—δὲ was throughout translated by them as "but," though this rendering in some cases completely spoiled the sense. I am glad, however, to be able to add that several showed acquaintance with the use of connecting particles. The answering in the History was, generally speaking, satisfactory.

PREPARATORY GRADE.—SECOND PAPER.—BOYS AND GIRLS.

Report of THOMAS W. DOUGAN, M.A.

I have examined the Second Paper of the Preparatory Grade, which contained prepared translation, translation at sight, and outlines of Grecian History.

A large percentage of the candidates showed signs of having been carefully prepared for the whole paper. Parsing is not, as a rule, done with sufficient precision; the person, number, tense, mood, and voice should, in the case of a finite verb, be specified. Most candidates are content with giving two or three of these particulars. Again "aorist" is not sufficient, there being two aorists.

Those who showed themselves well prepared in the prescribed translation usually did well also in the very similar passage for translation at sight.

The history questions were fairly answered by a large proportion of the students. Some showed that their memory had been more exercised than their reason: thus a large number gave *Attic* divisions in answer to the question "Into what classes was the population of Laconia divided?" and a great many confounded Cylon with Solon.

The work, however, was satisfactory on the whole, and gives evidence of much careful teaching.

LATIN.

SENIOR GRADE.—FIRST PAPER.—BOYS.

Report of LOUIS C. PURSER, D.LITT.

The work of the Senior Grade Boys was, on the whole, good. The answering in grammar was excellent, and most of the boys had a very fair conception of how to apply their knowledge in that branch to the writing of composition. The prose composition was better than I expected, as the passage set was full of grammatical difficulties. These were in most cases creditably surmounted, but there was noticeable a deficiency in Latin style, the sentences were not joined together and periods formed such as the Latin historians affect. Of course I must be understood to speak generally, for there were brilliant exceptions. Verse can hardly be said to exist. The Sallust was well prepared. Perhaps teachers might practice their pupils a little more in writing notes on difficult phrases. While appreciating the point in the phrase set for annotation, many good students expressed themselves either in too brief a fashion to be intelligible to anyone unless keenly alive to the answer, or else, after answering the question, wandered into discussions outside the topic altogether.

I must not fail to recognise, with gratitude, the excellent penmanship and general neatness displayed in the papers sent in by both boys and girls of both Senior and Middle Grades.

Senior Grade.—First Paper.—Girls.

Report of Louis C. Purser, D.Litt.

The Senior Grade Girls are, in my opinion, inferior on the whole to the boys; there is only one really promising scholar, I think, among them; the general level is mediocre. But still the answering was creditable, and hardly ever was signally bad. The grammar was good, prose composition passable, verse absolutely non-existent, translation quite satisfactory. They appear to have been well taught. Only forty-four were examined, a number too small to admit of generalizations of any real value.

Middle Grade.—First Paper.—Boys.

Report of Louis C. Purser, D.Litt.

The Middle Grade Boys are of many kinds. There are some who are of high promise; a large number who have fair abilities and are well taught; and there are very many who evidently make an effort, but who trust entirely to their memories and ought not to be taught classics at all. The answering in grammar is, as usual, good; but the application of grammar to composition not nearly so good on the whole as in the Senior Grade. The strange point about the compositions of the better class students is that, while they accurately understand really difficult points of grammar, such as indirect interrogative clauses, *oratio obliqua*, etc., they have a most defective feeling for the ordinary concords, *e.g.*, they write without hesitation *dui iussit* (this extraordinary construction was frequent and came from diverse centres); *spero, iudices, te visuros*, 'I hope, judges, that you will see.' The versifiers are few and far between, and have been treated with the utmost indulgence. The Cicero was very fairly done, considering the difficulty of the book; but there appears to me to be too much 'cramming up' of the author without adequate appreciation of the drift of his argument. I venture to think that teachers should, in the case of a speech like the *Pro Milone*, constantly ask their pupils to express the meaning and point of each successive passage in their own words. This would no doubt involve enormous labour during the first going-over of the speech, but would render the second study easier, and would certainly give a more intelligent knowledge of the real value of the work which is being read. This I say because I think that not five per cent. of the Middle Grade students really appreciated the argument in the second passage set.* Indeed, generally, I noticed far too large an amount of work that was unintelligent, long strings of words given which conveyed no meaning at all.

---

* *Pro Milone*, XXII. "In reum de servis . . . praedecti sunt."

MIDDLE GRADE.—FIRST PAPER.—GIRLS.

Report of LOUIS C. PURSER, D.LITT.

What has been said at the end of my report on the Middle Grade boys is still more true, in my opinion, of the girls. As a class, I should say that they certainly trust too much to their memories and too little to their intelligence; they do not know when they are ignorant of a thing. Here again brilliant exceptions (and there are four or five of them) must, of course, be excluded. The grammar is, as usual, good; the compositions fair; and the Cicero passable. One girl wrote a respectable set of verses.

JUNIOR GRADE.—FIRST PAPER.

Report of CHARLES H. KEENE, M.A., Rev. JAMES RICE, B.D., and Rev. GEORGE WILKINS, M.A.

The grammar questions were fairly done, though few candidates distinguished "*regĕre*" from "*regēre*" correctly.

The composition was in most cases indifferent, a large number of candidates failed to score thirty per cent.

The passages set for translation from the prescribed book (Caesar Bell. Gall. V.) were well done by many of the candidates. The translation of separate words from the same book was less satisfactory. Hardly any candidate gave the meaning of "*nam*," and many made very wild guesses at "*sudes*," "*senita*," "*cruciatus*," and "*materia*."

Some boys seemed not to know what is meant by the instruction to translate the first passage set, word for word, in "parallel columns."

Others again translated all the passages in this way instead of limiting themselves to the first as directed.

JUNIOR GRADE.—FIRST PAPER.—GIRLS.

Report of THOMAS W. DOUGAN, M.A.

The answering in grammar was better than that in composition. Many of the candidates were unable to make anything of the latter subject; many again showed that their studies had been extensive rather than accurate, putting forward French, Italian, Greek, and German words to do the work of Latin ones. When this device did not find favour hybrid words were freely coined. I had read several papers of this kind before I came across a really good one. On the whole it is true that there was a fair percentage of satisfactory papers, but I think the average of marks may be very considerably raised in coming years if more systematic attention is paid to composition.

The study of composition should, I think, proceed *pari passu* with the practice of translation from Latin into English. Some students and teachers tend to give too much *time* to composition: three separate hours per week are probably as good as six or nine; but no week (in the working part of the year) should elapse without its composition exercises.

PREPARATORY GRADE.—FIRST PAPER.—BOYS.

Report of Rev. JEREMIAH CROWE.

I have great pleasure in stating that the answering in this grade was, as a rule, highly satisfactory, in some cases it was even excellent, both in matter and in form. The improvement on former years is very marked. This is particularly the case in the answers to Grammar questions, which shows how well grounded boys have been in the foundations of the language. Students did not score so well in Composition as in Grammar. Although one is not prepared for equal scoring in both, yet it is somewhat remarkable that a boy who scores very highly in Grammar almost fails in Composition. Sometimes this was the case.

The prescribed author was carefully prepared; but one could not fail to notice the evidences of very frequent use of printed translations. I have invariably been obliged to mention how unsatisfactory the answers to questions in Geography have been: this year is no exception, and there appears to be little improvement on previous years. In many cases the answers have been nothing more than guesses; it is not desirable to develop a habit of that kind in youths. I should recommend more frequent use of maps, so that names of places occurring in the prescribed author may not be mere names to a boy, but may represent to him realities. I should also wish to recommend to teachers the desirability of attention to legible writing, to neatness, and to good arrangement. In many cases where the answers were substantially correct, there was a decided want under some of those heads, especially in the manner in which the answers to the Grammar questions were arranged. It would be well that teachers should call the attention of students to the necessity of writing the word for word translation in *parallel columns*. It is surprising the number of cases in which that simple and easy requirement was lost sight of.

PREPARATORY GRADE.—FIRST PAPER.—GIRLS.

Report of THOMAS W. DOUGAN, M.A.

I have examined these candidates in grammar, composition, and prepared extracts.

The prepared work appeared to have received careful attention from most candidates. The grammar was also on the whole very fairly done. More weakness was shown in composition than in any other part of the work; many candidates seemed never to have had any practice in this part of the work, and to make their maiden effort upon the examination sentences.

SENIOR GRADE.—SECOND PAPER.—BOYS AND GIRLS.

Report of R. C. B. KERIN, B.A.

The answering in this paper was extremely satisfactory. The renderings of the prescribed author were excellent in accuracy and style. Very few, however, were able to scan the Alcaic stanza. Some of the students showed great brilliancy in their translation of the rather difficult sight passage taken from the Epodes of Horace.* With the exception of question 6 (requiring explanations of the historical allusions in four quotations from Latin poets), the questions in History were treated clearly and intelligently.

MIDDLE GRADE.—SECOND PAPER.—BOYS.

Report of Rev. J. B. ARMOUR, M.A.

The answering all round was at least 15 per cent. higher than the same Grade in the second Latin paper three years ago. The failures were fewer, the style of answering was better, and the proportion of really good papers was greater. The unseen passages were tried by almost all, and as the

* Epode XVI., ll. 11-22.

translation of these is the real test of proficiency in Latin, it is but bare justice to the teachers as well as the taught to say that this part of the paper was specially well done. In many cases the rendering was excellent. The improvement in the answering on the Roman History was marked. The answering of the questions on parsing was perhaps the least satisfactory part of the paper. But taking the work as a whole, I am bound to report very favourably regarding the knowledge of the subject displayed in the answers. The charge against the Intermediate system of encouraging cramming has always been exaggerated, and the manner in which the passages for "translation at sight" were rendered proves it to have no foundation in fact.

Middle Grade.—Second Paper.—Girls.

Report of R. C. B. Kerin, B.A.

The papers were, on the whole, very satisfactory. Nearly all were successful in their translation of the passages taken from the prescribed author. The questions on the author were not so satisfactorily answered. Several ingenious guesses were made by the students who tried to distinguish *cassis* and *galea*, *scutum* and *clipeus*. Very few knew the real distinction.

The prose piece of sight translation was rendered in a very satisfactory manner. The verse passage, however, was not well done.

The answering of the History questions was deserving of the highest praise, but, in some cases, there was a tendency towards diffuseness and digression.

Junior Grade.—Second Paper.—Boys.

Report of Rev. D. Mannix, D.D., and Rev. Innocent Ryan.

We regard the answering of the boys as very satisfactory indeed. The percentage in marks is exceedingly high.

The fulness and accuracy of information, the facility and grace of expression, in the majority of cases, tell well for the training given in the Intermediate Schools.

The only notable deficiencies are in (*a*) prosody and scansion, and (*b*) in the grammar questions arising out of the text.

There are two portions of the business in which the pupils have scored splendidly—first, in the *subject-matter*, which is certainly thoroughly known; and second, in the "at sight translation," which, strange to say, is often satisfactorily done even by those who fail in the prescribed text.

Junior Grade.—Second Paper.—Girls.

Report of Rev. J. B. Armour, M.A.

The passages from the prescribed authors were well rendered in point of accuracy and style; the parsing of the words was very fair, and the answering in Roman History was good. The extracts for "translation at sight" were very well done in the majority of cases, and by about a third of the candidates, in a manner which indicated a knowledge of Latin surprisingly high for girls of 16 years of age. I had no opportunity of examining any papers of boys of the Junior Grade, but I may say the boys did well if their papers all round were superior to those submitted to me. In some of the questions on Roman History a slight tendency to a round-about style of answering was noticeable; but, as a whole, the answering was direct, accurate, and good, indicating careful preparation on the part of the pupils, and earnest work by the teachers. The papers were the best I have yet examined of the girls in the Junior Grade.

PREPARATORY GRADE.—SECOND PAPER.—BOYS.

Report of Very Rev. J. J. KELLY.

I am glad to report that the answering of the Preparatory boys, in general, was decidedly better than that of last year. Generally speaking, every part of the paper, translation of set passages, parsing, the subject-matter, translation of unprepared passages, was better answered. Many candidates got full marks and a majority got a high percentage for translation of the passages from the prepared selections. The part of the examination which pleased me most was the translation of the unprepared passages, which, after composition, I consider to be the best test of a real knowledge of the language. A few of the candidates got almost full marks for the translation of the unseen passages, prose and verse, many got very high marks, and almost half got fifty per cent. I consider this highly creditable to boys so young, and from my experience of last year, I was agreeably surprised at the successful attempts of the Preparatory boys, in this the most trying part of the paper.

The knowledge of scansion, and the quantities of syllables, shown in answers to question (4)* was not, on the whole, satisfactory.

The weakest part in the answering was the parsing, conjugation of verbs, and declension of nouns occurring in the passages set.

The question on the subject-matter of the selections, was, on the whole, well answered.

The Roman History was, on the whole, fairly known; but in some papers there was evidence that there had been no regular continuous study of the history, and that it had been attempted to get up a smattering of it in a short time.

The orthography was, in general, good; the penmanship in many cases excellent, in nearly all clearly legible; the answers in most of the papers, carefully arranged, and the papers on the whole very creditable to boys so young.

I think much labour and practice on the part of pupils, and continual instruction and correction on the part of teachers, must have been given to the translation of unprepared passages, and they have been well repaid.

I would suggest more attention to parsing and the necessity of requiring the pupils to parse every word in a passage fully, and not merely those words which present some special difficulty.

Prosody requires more attention.

I am satisfied that the examination of the Preparatory boys, second paper, shows a striking improvement on that of last year, and is very creditable to the boys themselves, and to the masters of the schools in which they were prepared.

PREPARATORY GRADE.—SECOND PAPER.—GIRLS.

Report of Rev. J. B. ARMOUR, M.A.

As an indication of the progress made in matters educational since the establishment of the Intermediate system, I may say that these papers in the Preparatory Grade were quite as good this year as the corresponding papers in the Junior Grade were four years ago. The prescribed passages were well translated, and the course must have been all read

---

* (4). "Scan, marking the division of feet and the quantity of each syllable:—
(a.) Quid non saeva sibi voluit Fortuna licere?
Aut ubi non mors est, si jugulatis aquae?"

by the majority of the pupils, as the concluding lines were set, and were in almost all cases translated. The parsing was very good, the scansion of the lines set was fair, and the answering on Roman History was satisfactory. The prose passage for "translation at sight" was very generally attempted, and the meaning in many cases was well brought out. The passage of poetry was not so well done, but to set a passage of poetry was an experiment, and I think the experiment should be repeated. The papers were very creditable in every way and deserve praise.

ENGLISH.

Senior Grade.—First Paper.—Boys.

Report of William Magennis, m.a.

It affords me no little gratification to be able to report that the English Compositions of the Senior Grade boys were in very many cases admirable. The fact that so many boys have been trained to such a degree of excellence is an eloquent tribute to the Intermediate schools of the country, and a striking testimony to the nature of their work. The majority of the candidates elected to write upon "The Value of Examination as a Test of Educational Proficiency," and of these many, unfortunately, strayed from the point and discussed the value of examination as an incentive to study, and enlarged upon the superiority of Competitive Examination for public posts over the older system of selection. The compositions which dealt with "The Disadvantages of the Multiplication of Books and Periodical Literature" were, almost without exception, exceedingly good; and quite a large number of them exhibited a surprisingly close acquaintance with the current literature of the day. Of the very few which had for their text a passage from the speech of Bassanio on the choice of the caskets, scarcely one deserved honourable mention; platitudes about hypocrisy, and the deceptiveness of appearance, were the staple ingredients; and the literary workmanship was poor.

The "Merchant of Venice" was, on the whole, well prepared, though but little attention would seem to have been paid to Shakesperian grammar. Indeed the answering in grammar was somewhat unsatisfactory. Scarcely a score of candidates could give an intelligent account of what they understand by the term "Parts of Speech," and make their account harmonise with the recognition of the Interjection as a part of speech. Philology and Prosody appear to have been more or less neglected studies, whereas Analysis of complex sentences has been done to perfection.

Senior Grade.—First Paper.—Girls.

Report of William Magennis, m.a.

The girl candidates in Senior Grade are a marked improvement upon those of last year. I must, however, repeat as regards a large section of them much of what I had to remark about their predecessors: they display a want of training not merely in Composition but in the work of answering questions coherently, intelligibly, and concisely. Quite a considerable number wrote essays upon the text from Shakespeare that might with equal fitness have been appended to any other text. Echoes of religious instruction, and the common phrases of common conversation, such as "Everyone, rich or poor, high or low," "Of no service to himself or to anyone else," "If a man wishes to succeed in this life," serve the purpose of expanding vapid essays to the length of some seven or eight pages, a length which the writers seem to believe is demanded by the examiner. Very few of this year's candidates indulged in the practice of substituting questions of their own for those on the paper; but some entirely misunderstood the purport of the question:—"Write a brief sketch of the character of Bassanio." They gave an epitome of the "Pound of Flesh Plot," an estimate of Antonio, and a eulogy of Portia, but no words concerning Bassanio himself further than that he was "a profligate, and he didn't deserve Portia." The questions requiring quotations and notes were, as a rule, well done; indeed the general average was higher in respect of these questions than in respect of those which demanded more of original work. As in the case of the Senior boys analysis was well done; and—as was not the case with the Senior boys—the description of the Spenserian stanza rarely failed to get good marks.

It is a pity that more effort is not made to cultivate the reasoning powers of the girl students. They suffer more from deficiency in reasoning at these examinations than from weakness of memory. Their answers too frequently contain a mass of matter, valuable as information, but irrelevant: and their relevant answers as frequently lack form. The girls have not the same wealth of ideas as the boys, nor the same capacity for order and system in their work, though they not seldom have more fluency, and display a better acquaintance with the annotations of the prescribed text.

Middle Grade.—First Paper.—Boys.

Report of Rev. Henry Evans, D.D.

The answering of the boys in the subject matter of the First English paper indicates a fair degree of progress. This is apparent both as regards the knowledge exhibited and the style in which it is set forth.

The *compositions* are mostly good; they are shorter than usual, but the order of thought is generally logical, and the language fairly appropriate. There are fewer errors in orthography, fewer colloquial expressions, and fewer grotesque statements than formerly. Excessive rehearsal of hackneyed stories is the most frequent fault.

Compared with former years, the answering in *grammar* shows improvement; but it is still weak. Parsing is the least satisfactory part of the work done within the limits of this paper. About one-third only of the candidates may be said to have parsed *fully*.

The work done in the department of *analysis* exhibits growing progress. The functions of the various members of a sentence are intelligently understood by a large proportion of the candidates, and the power to state the nature of the relations in which the several parts or phrases stand to each other is possessed by many. There is evident painstaking in the teaching of this subject.

The answering in *Paradise Lost*, Book VII., reaches a high standard, especially in making the required quotations from the text. A good deal of attention has evidently been given to the structure of the metre and to scansion. Quite a number of the candidates give evidence of satisfactory acquaintance with this subject. They can fairly exemplify the characteristics of Milton's verse by comparing *Paradise Lost* with extracts from Shakespeare. The possession of this power will enable them to make better progress in future.

Middle Grade.—First Paper.—Girls.

Report of Rev. Henry Evans, D.D.

The essays written by the girls of the Middle Grade do not display a high average capacity in the art of English composition. They exhibit fluency of diction, and considerable versatility in drawing from memory, but too often the matter lacks sequence, and is redundant in anecdote. Some compositions, it is true, possess much merit; not many that of originality.

In *grammar* the average answering is on much the same level as that of the boys. Not many sufficiently know the irregular comparison of adjectives, but those who do possess this knowledge set it forth admirably.

Most of the candidates seem to possess a satisfactory acquaintance with the principles and methods of *analysis*. Even those whose work is not the best, show evidence of knowing how to approach the resolving of a sentence into its component parts. Lack of orderliness in exhibiting analysis too often disfigures work otherwise well done.

The chief feature of the answering in Book VII. of *Paradise Lost* appears in the fulness and readiness with which the candidates are able to rehearse the text. Quotation is copiously made, and frequently in the very order of the lines on the original page. Memory, too, does more than its share in the explanation of passages and particular uses of words, such explanation, for the most part, being simply a reproduction of the notes contained in the annotated editions of Milton which the students read. Although the answering of the girls in regard to metre and scansion is not equal to that of the boys, it is on the whole quite creditable and often excellent. In the knowledge of metre and verse structure there is hopeful progress.

Junior Grade.—First Paper.—Boys.

Report of Rev. L. A. Barry, LL.D., John Cooke, M.A., Robert Donovan, B.A., and William Macinnis, M.A.

The compositions were, in the majority of cases, fairly good; some, indeed, were excellent. The prevailing fault was defective punctuation; nor were instances wanting of bad grammar, bad spelling, and slip-shod English.

In grammar the answering was not at all satisfactory. Analysis seems to have been a comparatively neglected study this year; and parsing, apparently, fared little better. Many boys confounded the *complement* with the *adverbial extension* of the predicate, and even the predicate with the subject; some, too, parsed "amiss" as a preposition, and "whose" as nominative case.

The faults in the sentences given for correction* were in nearly every case detected, but the reasons assigned for the corrections proposed were not always just or sufficient.

---

* "Correct the following faulty sentences, and in each case give your reason for the correction:—

"(a.) I have begun Euclid yesterday, but I did not begin Algebra yet.
"(b.) Nobody put themselves out of their way to convenience him.
"(c.) That is the man whom I perceived was in fault.
"(d.) I am after losing my pen.
"(e.) Paper burns quicker nor cloth."

The prescribed cantos of Scott's "Lord of the Isles" were evidently not neglected in the schools. The questions dealing with them were usually well answered. The repetition, however, of certain passages displayed in too many cases an equal disregard for the meaning and the metre.

JUNIOR GRADE.—FIRST PAPER.—GIRLS.

Report of DANIEL CROLY, M.A.

The paper contained three groups of questions. (a.) Composition, (b.) Grammar, and (c.) Scott's Lord of the Isles, Cantos I., II., III.

(a.) Of the subjects set for the composition the first, "What profession or business would you like to adopt, and why?", was most frequently selected; the second "the importance of trifles," was taken by a large number, and the third subject "Slow rises Worth by Poverty depressed" was treated by very few.

The essays were fairly done, and showed a decided improvement on last year. The absolute failures were few. The chief faults were bad punctuation and unnecessarily long sentences.

(b.) The answering in grammar was poor in very many cases. Only a few candidates succeeded in getting high marks on the question, and yet the sentences given were simple and easy.

The parsing was not sufficiently full or complete. Many of the answers seemed to be mere guesses, and the relation of each word parsed to other words in the sentence was not clearly shown or explained.

The correction of the faulty sentences was good all round, and the reasons for the corrections were given more generally than usual.

Many failed to draw the distinction between the uses of the relative pronouns *who* and *which*, and confounded relative pronouns with interrogative pronouns.

(c.) The answers to the questions on Scott's Lord of the Isles showed that the poem had been well and carefully prepared. The extracts prescribed were fully explained, and as usual the text was known well by rote.

PREPARATORY GRADE.—FIRST PAPER.—BOYS.

Report of P. W. JOYCE, LL.D., and J. PATERSON SMYTH, LL.D.

Last year's examiners of this Grade complained of the candidates' deficiency in punctuation; management of capital letters; manner of writing poetry, and of striking out or inserting words; and other such matters. In all these particulars there is this year a very obvious improvement, that is to say, the errors complained of, though by no means eradicated, are much less general this year than last. The grammar is decidedly better, and the majority of the candidates did their parsing well.

Many of the candidates lost marks heavily, and some failed altogether, in this part of their examination, from not attending to the directions given on the question paper. Thus, instead of writing a single composition on one of the three subjects given for choice, some wrote on two, and a few on the whole three. Instead of parsing the ten italicised words, as they were told to do, some parsed—or attempted to parse—all the words in the five passages given—fifty-six words altogether. A considerable number committed this last blunder.

A great many candidates deliberately answered more than they were asked: probably in their anxiety to do well, and some perhaps to show how much they knew. This merely wastes the candidate's time, troubles the examiner, and goes for nothing. The examiner reads through a whole page of weary irrelevant matter, and at last lights on the answer, consisting perhaps of half a dozen words.

Candidates should learn to spell the names of their text-book authors. A large number gave Thomas Moore as "*Moor*"; some made him "Sir Thomas Moore," and some "Thomas O'Moore." Campbell figures as *Campell*, *Cambell*, and *Camble*; and Sir Samuel Ferguson as *Fergison*, *Fergurson*, *Fergusion*, *Fergusloin*, &c. Common grammatical terms were extremely often mis-spelled:—*Nomitive case*, *nomative*, *nuter gendre*, &c. Indeed the mis-spelling was not confined to grammatical terms and the names of authors. In a large proportion of the papers the spelling of ordinary English words was very bad.

Composition and explanation of subject-matter continue to be the weak points. Though we got a fair number of good essays, we consider the composition, on the whole, decidedly disappointing, a very large number scoring not more than twenty per cent. of the allotted marks.

Preparatory Grade.—First Paper.—Girls.

Report of C. F. Bastable, LL.D.

The answering all round was much better than I had expected, and compared most favourably with that of the Junior Grade of some years ago.

The compositions were fair, and though none reached a high standard of excellence there were not many bad failures.

One of the grammar questions—that on the pluperfect tense*—gave a good deal of trouble to most candidates, but the parsing was creditable.

In the select poetry the average answering was high; the text had been carefully made up, and most of the papers were neatly turned out, clean and well arranged.

One curious defect may be noticed, viz.:—the wrong spelling of some common grammatical terms. Even in otherwise very good papers I met with "nomative," "interroggative," or "relltive." A little attention would remedy this fault.

Senior Grade.—Second Paper.—Boys.

Report of Robert Donovan, M.A.

The answering of the Senior Grade boys to the questions on Scott's "Waverley," the History of Great Britain and Ireland, Geography, and the History of English Literature was, on the whole, good.

The papers on "Waverley" were especially satisfactory. It is often urged as a reason against the selection of such a book for examination purposes, that the pleasure of reading is wholly destroyed by the necessity for a minute and careful study of the text. The answers of the candidates in this Grade showed how little ground there is for the contention. The papers that exhibited the most careful study of the text, even of its dialectic peculiarities in style and words, were precisely those papers which also gave evidence of the keenest appreciation of the humour, character, and artistic qualities of the story. It is quite plain that the study of "Waverley" by the candidates for this examin-

* "Describe the use of the pluperfect tense, and give one example in a short sentence containing the verbs [illegible] and go."

ation was a task of pleasure; and that it must have tended to develop a healthy literary taste and sound critical judgment among them.

The answering to the questions on *History* was also good; but was open to improvement in the direction of greater fullness and accuracy. Senior Grade candidates should not, in an enumeration of the causes of the American War of Independence, omit all reference to the consequences of the annulling of the Massachusetts Charter. And in narrating a series of incidents so greatly affected in its course by party changes and the personal influence of ministers, such as Grenville, Rockingham, Townsend, Pitt, and North, confusion as to these changes and the personal responsibility of the various ministers in the different developments of policy should not exist. It is to miss some of the most valuable lessons of history to be uninformed on such points or unappreciative of their significance. The questions on *Irish History* were, in most cases, well answered, though some of the candidates were unprepared for examination in the chapters on the literature and institutions of Ancient Ireland.

The questions on the *Geography* of the American Continent were fairly answered. Few of the candidates, however, displayed an accurate knowledge of the historical, political, or commercial causes of the prominence of the cities and towns which they were asked to locate. When facts of this kind are ignored, the study of geography loses almost all its interest and a great part of its value. The answering to the first part of question 11—"Give the real time of the earth's rotation on its axis. Explain the difference between a Sidereal and a Solar day"—was bad. It was surprising what a large number of intelligent and otherwise well informed boys gave as an answer to the first part of this question—"365 days, 5 hours, and a fraction"; while only a few attempted any answer to the second part. It might be urged that such questions and the subjects of the programme under which they fall are not properly included under the science of geography. But whatever name be given to the study of elementary facts concerning the movements of the earth, the causes of day and night, and the measurement of time, it would be regrettable if the best students of the Intermediate Schools remained wholly ignorant of them. The papers also proved that a more extensive use of the Atlas by the students in their study of the subject would be desirable.

The period of English literary history appointed for examination was apparently studied with care by most of the boys. Few of the candidates, however, were able to give any account of Dryden's prose works. Regarding a writer of prose, whose fame rests chiefly on his poetry, that want of knowledge might be to some extent explicable, although inexcusable in the case of "the father of English Criticism." But many of the candidates in attempting to answer the question gave the names of his didactic poems instead of his essays; and seemed to be under the impression that such works as the "Hind and the Panther" and the "Religio Laici" were written in prose. A blunder of this kind should be impossible in the case of an intelligent student. But it illustrates one of the defects involved in any routine study of the subject from a manual, when not illustrated by some direct knowledge of the books of which the names and dates are being mechanically learned. This mistake, which was common to a large number of the papers, was the chief blemish of this part of the examination. On the other hand, the question on Shakespeare's dramatic method* was answered by a very

* "In the work of delineating passion and feeling Shakespeare proceeds as only the greatest dramatic authors can." Explain.

large number of the candidates in a manner that showed not merely their acquaintance with the text-book, but also their understanding of an abstruse piece of literary criticism. Some of the candidates exemplified the truth of this criticism and of the comparison made in another chapter of the text-book between Scott and Shakespeare, by apposite references to "Waverley" and "The Merchant of Venice." Such answers indicated that in these cases, the study of literary history was not a mere exercise of the memory, but a training in literary criticism and its methods as well.

Senior Grade.—Second Paper.—Girls.

Report of Robert Donovan, M.A.

The observations made in the report on the examination of the Senior Grade Boys in this paper apply almost without qualification to the examination of the Girl candidates.

The papers would gain in merit if the answers were more concise and direct. If any further addition to the remarks on the Boys' papers has to be made, it must be by way of increased praise. The Girls' papers on Scott and History impressed me as fuller in detail, more accurate, and more appreciative of the picturesque and romantic elements in both the story and the history. Geography was not so carefully studied; otherwise the papers, as a whole, were creditable.

Middle Grade.—Second Paper.—Boys.

Report of Henry S. Macran, M.A.

The answering on Lamb's Essays was, generally speaking, very disappointing. The questions on the meanings of words and phrases were answered well enough, but the candidates for the most part seemed to have absolutely no appreciation of Lamb's humour and pathos, and, in attempting to quote passages, omitted every delicate touch.

The answering in History and Geography Proper was very good; the maps were well done; and there was a distinct improvement in Physical Geography.

The answering on the History of English Literature was poor, and many candidates attempted none of the questions.

Middle Grade.—Second Paper.—Girls.

Report of Henry S. Macran, M.A.

The answering of the girls on Lamb's Essays was very satisfactory, and contrasted most favourably with that of the boys. A large proportion of the candidates seemed to have fully appreciated the literary characteristics of the author, and not to have studied him merely as a storehouse of obsolete words and curious phrases.

The answering in History and Geography proper was very fair; the maps were good; and the History of English Literature was well prepared.

The prolixity, which was such a painful feature of the girls' answering last year, was barely visible on this occasion.

It is strange that Lamb's Essays, which seem so unsuitable as a study for young boys, seem at the same time well adapted for girls. The answering of the latter showed a distinct appreciation of the literary side of the author.

JUNIOR GRADE.—SECOND PAPER.—BOYS.

Report of KATHARINE MURPHY, M.A., and Rev. PATRICK O'LEARY.

The papers, on the whole, show careful and intelligent preparation; the majority are fair, some are remarkably good, and only very few are decidedly bad.

The penmanship is, as a rule, good. The spelling is fair, except in the case of geographical names; but more attention ought to be paid to the use of capitals and punctuation.

The "Robinson Crusoe" seems to have been studied carefully.

The answering in Geography is good; we must, however, except the answer to the question in Physical Geography,* which is rarely satisfactory.

The English History is somewhat defective; the sketches of the career of Cardinal Wolsey are inaccurate, and the treatment of other questions, even when accurate, is meagre: for instance, as a statement of the result of the first battle of St. Alban's, something more is expected than "Yorkists won"—the general answer given.

But by far the least satisfactory part of the examination is the Irish History; very many make no attempt to answer the questions, whilst of those who do make an attempt, the majority score nothing, or practically nothing and comparatively few get full, or even half marks.

JUNIOR GRADE.—SECOND PAPER.—GIRLS.

Report of R. J. SEMPLE, M.A.

The second English paper, Junior Grade, consisted of three parts—(1) Robinson Crusoe, Defoe; (2) Geography; (3) English and Irish History; and as the answering on these three sections varied considerably, even in the case of the same pupils, I shall, for convenience, consider each part separately, and then give a general view of the answering as a whole.

I. Taking first the questions on Robinson Crusoe,† I soon found that where description and general facts were required these were, for the most part, fairly well answered; but where details were asked, they were rarely given accurately. For instance, while Questions 1, 4, and 5 (*a*) and (*b*), which imply a general acquaintance with the book, were as a rule well answered, the remaining questions, which require a more minute knowledge of the text, were often missed. Question 2 (*a*) was only answered by a very few, and even these rarely gave a

---

* "Account for the moist and comparatively equable climate of Ireland."

† "1. Describe briefly the circumstances of Crusoe's escape from Sallee.

"2. (*a*.) How did Crusoe manage to light a fire on the island?

"(*b*.) How did he make and bake bread?

"(*c*.) What material had he for candles?

"3. 'There was a strange concurrence of days in the various providences which befell me.' Explain.

"4. (*a*.) Describe briefly Crusoe's first sickness on the island, and the remedy he discovered for this disorder.

"(*b*.) Recount the 'terrible dream' which accompanied this attack.

"5. (*a*.) What instructions did the Spaniard receive before crossing to the main to rescue his comrades?

"(*b*.) What seasonable advice had he previously given Crusoe?

"(*c*.) What arms and ammunition did Crusoe provide for this undertaking?"

satisfactory explanation; while Question 5 (c) was almost left unnoticed by the more cautious, or wildly guessed at by the more confident. As to Question 3, while a great number of students gave the proper concurrences, very many failed to express their meaning in a clear and intelligent form. In some cases also students lost much time by answering in too minute detail questions which expressly required a brief description. While reading this section of the papers I could not help thinking that teachers would secure much better results if they more frequently held written examinations on the text-books, as in this manner students would necessarily learn accuracy and freedom of expression, and, at the same time, they would acquire that grasp of leading facts and circumstances which any brief description must require.

II. When we come to Geography, the second main division of the paper, it was at once apparent that the questions which imply a minute and accurate acquaintance with the towns and rivers of the three kingdoms were, as a rule, satisfactorily answered, while those which deal with the situation and capitals of the colonies, the principal mountains, lakes, and rivers of Africa, were sometimes entirely overlooked, or more frequently attempted in such a way as to display the gross ignorance of the pupils in this most important department of Geography. The average student was well acquainted with Questions 7, 8, and 9,* but made only ludicrous guesses at the situation of Tasmania, the capital of New Zealand, or the river on which Calcutta is situated. While great numbers could tell the exact position of the Mersey and the Moy, they failed to give a single river in Europe or America flowing into the Arctic Ocean. Physical Geography appears to have shared the fate of the general geography of the world, and seems to have been entirely neglected in the schools, or very imperfectly taught. The more extensive use of maps of the world, and the frequent exercise of students in pointing out lakes, rivers, and mountains would have obviated most of the grosser blunders, and would have fittingly prepared pupils for that more particular acquaintance with the Geography of the British Isles, which seems to have engrossed the first and largest portion of the time devoted to this important subject.

III. The questions on the last section of the paper are divided into those on English and those on Irish History. The answering on the former was admirable all through, and evinced careful preparation. The 14th question† of course brought out the best students, but nearly all gave a fair account of the career of the great Cardinal, while even the most backward pupils had an exact acquaintance with the battles of the Wars of the Roses, and showed an intelligent appreciation of the character of the hero of Agincourt and of the fate of the King-maker. But when we turn to the department of Irish History the tale is entirely different. Some students undoubtedly gave considerable attention to this most important branch of History with the best results. But the general verdict is not altered by these exceptions. A great number of even the best students in other respects failed to secure a single mark in Irish History, and in too many cases the attempt to answer these questions showed the hasty and imperfect manner in which Irish History is taught in many of our schools.

* "7. In what counties are the following places situated:—Tunbridge Wells, Epsom, Peterhead, Kilkee, Kinsale?

"8. Between what counties do the following rivers enter the sea:—Mersey, Dee (Scotch), Thames, Humber, Lagan, and Moy?

"9. Name the inland counties of Connaught and Munster, with their chief towns."

† "14. Sketch shortly the career of Cardinal Wolsey."

When we consider the answering as a whole, we cannot fail to be favourably impressed with the small number of papers which display gross illiteracy, or which betray complete ignorance of the subjects of examination. History, Geography, and the prescribed text-book seem to have been studied carefully during the year, and while one part of the course may have been unduly exalted at the expense of another, yet, as a rule, the answering is fair in every branch. But while there are a number who have brought credit on themselves and their teachers by superior answering in one or all of the divisions of the paper, yet I think the average is not so high as the extent of the course, the training of the pupils, and the comparative easiness of the questions would lead one to expect.

Preparatory Grade.—Second Paper.—Boys.

Report of Rev. J. B. M'Bride, B.A., Rev. Daniel O'Loan, and Rev. J. Edgar Henry, M.A.

The general answering of the Preparatory Grade, Boys, in the second English paper was very good, especially when the tender years of many of them are taken into consideration. The greater number showed that they clearly understood the questions asked, and displayed intelligence, if not always accuracy, in answering those which they attempted. But while bearing this testimony to the answering of the great majority of the boys, we must say that a number—far too large a number—gave evidence of somewhat defective training. Some seem to be quite unfamiliar with the manner in which questions should be answered. Instead of answering directly, and in a few words, such questions as "When and where did Crusoe become a sailor, a slave," &c.! quite a number of boys wrote down all they could remember of Crusoe's career from the time he left home until he was cast on the uninhabited island, omitting moreover from their narrative the only matters to which the question had reference.

Another section of boys displayed a total absence of reflection on the meaning of what they wrote. Some answers were merely incoherent echoes of half remembered sentences, having no apparent meaning whatever, and others were so obviously self contradictory, or contrary to the nature of things, that it is plain the authors wrote without any thought whatever. In giving the dates, *e.g.*, of Crusoe's birth, going to sea, and landing on the island, some boys make him an able-bodied seaman and a shipwrecked mariner a considerable time before his birth, others in the very year of his birth, and others again in his infancy or childhood; whilst several put a period of nearly two centuries between the one event and the other. Similar want of reflection was shown in giving the dates of the first coming of the Danes to Ireland, and of their final overthrow at Clontarf, the latter event being often placed several hundred years earlier than the former. Such training as these students have received is not education; they have never been taught to use their reasoning powers.

In our opinion it would be well if in all schools the practice were adopted of holding written examinations occasionally, in order to exercise the pupils in framing coherent and concise answers to plain questions.

PREPARATORY GRADE.—SECOND PAPER.—GIRLS.

Report of J. EDGAR HENRY, M.A.

Whether as regards substance or form, the answering in this group of subjects must be characterized as good. In almost all cases there has been careful preparation of the entire course, and answers are put in fair literary form. Both spelling and composition are well done as a rule, and absolute illiteracy is rare. As might be expected, the poorest answers are those which involve a process of induction, whilst the memorizing has been most thorough. The summarising is often indifferent, but marks a slight improvement on former years.

In Geography the best answering is on the map of Ireland, and the second best on the map of the world.

Very few of the candidates show acquaintance with the sub-divisions of magnitude, &c., indicated on the map of the world.

As regards order and neatness, there is a marked improvement on former years, the questions being in almost all cases correctly numbered and treated consecutively, and the answer to each completed in the part of the book where it is begun.

COMMERCIAL ENGLISH.

SENIOR AND MIDDLE GRADES.—BOYS AND GIRLS.

Report of JOHN COOKE, M.A.

SENIOR GRADE.

The exercise in copying manuscript was in this Grade satisfactorily done, and showed much care had been taken in the preparation for it. The writing of some however was not good, and the same defects were noted as in the Middle Grade.

The Geography questions were not very well answered, particularly questions 1 and 4.* In the latter, some went into the relative merits of the railway system and shipping, instead of confining their answers strictly to the comparative positions of the two countries in these respects.

The answering in History† was however more satisfactory. Question 5 was fairly well answered. Many mistook the drift of question 6, and few stated the colonies correctly in answer to the latter half of the question. Some repeated portions of the answer to question 7 in their answers to question 8, and most seemed to have attempted question 9 hastily, failing to make a complete statement.

---

* "1. Mention in the order of their importance the chief regions of production for (a) gold, (b) silver, and give some facts as to the relative amounts of these metals produced in recent years.

"4. Compare the position of the United Kingdom with that of the United States in respect to (a) coal production; (b) exports; (c) imports; (d) merchant shipping; (e) railway mileage."

† "5. Narrate briefly the origin and early progress of the East India Company. Who was Sir Josiah Child?

"6. Give some account of the main features of British commerce about the middle of the 17th century. What colonies did England possess at that time?

"7. Describe the general character of British colonial policy in the 18th century, and give some examples of its application.

"8. Estimate the gains and losses of English trade during the great wars with France (1793–1815).

"9. A series of new influences began to affect industry and commerce about 1850. State what these influences were, and point out their general effect."

Middle Grade.

The exercise in copying manuscript was satisfactorily done on the whole. There was evidence that practice in this portion of the subject had been given. The writing however of many was not good, nor in a style suited for business purposes. The use of the mark [denoting a fresh paragraph was frequently misunderstood, and the notes on the margin denoting corrections were sometimes inserted in the copy as portion of the text.

The Geography questions were not so well answered. In questions 1 and 4,* dealing with such well known products as sugar and silk, many failed to give even an average answer. Question 2† also was not well answered; and some, more particularly the girls, showed little idea of not only what an acre meant in size, but also of the proportion of tilled to untilled land in Ireland.

The questions in History were however better answered, and showed that the text books had been read with some care.

Junior Grade.—Boys and Girls.

Report of C. F. Bastable, ll.d.

The answering in this grade was decidedly unsatisfactory. With a few exceptions, the copying exercises showed great want of intelligence. Instead of seeking to discover the general meaning of the passage set, most of the candidates guessed at the separate words, making the most amusing mistakes in the attempt.

The geography—much the easiest part of the work—was better done than the history, but did not come near the proper standard.

About three-fourths of the candidates failed to answer any of the history questions, and evidently had not the least idea of what commercial history is.

A good many of the answer books were badly arranged, and the spelling was poor.

PRÉCIS.

Senior and Middle Grades.

Report of Robert Donovan, m.a.

The results of the examination in Précis writing were not satisfactory. Though the programme of examinations clearly defines the object, the proper form, and the merits of a Précis, a very large number of the candidates seem to have been totally uninformed on these elementary points.

Many of them prepared, instead of a Précis, an index, letter by letter and date by date, to the correspondence. Others set out, letter by letter, in minute detail, the unimportant as well as the important matters contained therein. Some repeated the same fact three times in their narrative, referring first to a telegram, next to a letter covering an enclosure, and finally to the enclosure. Where condensation was

* "1. In what parts of the British Empire is sugar largely produced? Show the commercial importance of this product, and state the chief places from which the United Kingdom obtains its supplies.

"4. (a.) Give the principal seats in the United Kingdom of the manufacture of silk. Whence is the raw product obtained?

"(b.) What special manufactures are carried on at Benares, Bombay, Calcutta?"

† "2. State approximately the acreage of Ireland devoted to the culture of barley, oats, potatoes, and wheat respectively. How does Ireland compare with Great Britain in respect to each of these crops?"

attempted the candidates too often failed to distinguish what was essential from what was unessential to an adequate record. The papers that gave evidence of sound training in Précis writing were a minority. Even the minority would be improved by greater attention to style and precision. Legibility and neatness are qualities to be looked for in an exercise of this kind; and in these qualities the papers were also open to improvement.

These criticisms are general; but are more fully applicable to the Middle Grade papers than to the Senior. Even among the latter, however, there were altogether too many candidates who were ignorant even of the form a Précis should take.

It should be added after so much fault-finding that some of the papers, though too few to do general credit to the schools, were the work of carefully trained and intelligent candidates. Should the standard attained by these candidates become general or be approached by the general level of work in this branch of the Intermediate course, the result will be creditable to the schools and most valuable as an educational achievement. An exercise that develops in the pupil habits of concise and exact expression, and trains him in the discernment of the important and essential from the unimportant and accidental in the matter he reads, is certain to have effects on his general intelligence and his capacity for the rapid and permanent acquirement of knowledge in many directions.

FRENCH.

Senior Grade.—Boys.

Report of F. J. Amours.

Out of the six questions on Grammar, the first and third* have brought out the best answers. The sixth†, dealing with the derivation of French words, seems to have been unexpected by most of the candidates, as only fifteen of them gained more than half the marks allotted to it. The difference between the pluperfect and the past anterior (question 4)‡ proved a stumbling block to nine-tenths of the pupils, and the same haziness as to the use of the various past tenses is also prevalent in the Composition, which however is fairly well done. The idiomatical phrases reach about the usual standard. L'Invasion has been carefully read, although too many candidates are of opinion that Geneviève de Brabant is the name of a celebrated lady novelist. Polyeucte is often translated too literally; pupils should be cautioned early against rendering French words by English words of the same origin; *présumer, trépas, tourmentés* are not exactly equivalent to *presume, trespass, tormented*. Both the unseen extracts are very well done.

---

* "1. Write the following sentences with the negatives *ne . . . pas* added to the principal verb, and give rules for the changes that must take place in the secondary clause:—

"(a.) *Je suis certain qu'il viendra.*
"(b.) *Je crains qu'il n'arrive trop tard.*
"(c.) *Je crois qu'il faudrait finir.*
"(d.) *Je doute qu'il le fasse.*

"3. Give the adverb, one noun and one verb formed from the following adjectives:—*ample, faible, fou, franc, gai, lent, patient, précis, profond, triste.* Add the meaning of every word."

† "6. Derive from French elements the words *fainéant, hormis, naguère, nonchalant, [illegible].*"

‡ "4. Explain clearly and illustrate by examples the difference between the pluperfect and the past anterior after such expressions as *dès que* or *lorsque*."

SENIOR GRADE.—GIRLS.

Report of F. J. AMOURS.

My remarks on the Senior Boys' paper apply in every particular to those of the Senior Girls with the important addition that in every part of the paper, questions, composition and translation, the girls have reached a better percentage of marks, and consequently the number of Honours and Passes is slightly higher, and the failures about five per cent. lower.

MIDDLE GRADE.—BOYS and GIRLS.

Report of G. E. BARBIER.

As regards the composition, which is the chief test of the examination, notwithstanding the apparently weak results all round, the impression left on my mind is that the results are satisfactory. I have very clearly noticed that more time and more attention have been devoted to this branch of the examination. When I say "satisfactory," I do not mean "excellent." I mean that, taking the average, the composition was of sufficient merit to secure a pass, and showed much improvement upon the composition read by me in the Middle Grade in former years.

A good many candidates failed who had evidently devoted some time to a part of their set work, but who turned out a translation disconnected in several parts as to sense, and, in truth, meaning nothing on the whole. This was chiefly the case in the passage from Racine.

I will draw attention to a feature noticeable every year within about the same dimensions, but which may be brought advantageously under principals' and students' notice alike.

Some students, well up in grammar, think that they are bound to pass if they answer two or three questions of that subject, with the intention of hurrying to a part of the paper they like better, for example the translation from the French. They are clever students and they could pass easily, if they would devote a little more attention to the grammar. They think they have done enough of this part of the examination for a pass, but they are frequently mistaken.

The writing has been very clear and pleasing on the whole. Among some of the better papers, however, the writing has been bad, very bad, and the examiner used a good deal of indulgence and patience to correct them, but, notwithstanding his absolute sense of fairness, it is very plain that a badly written paper is bound to lose marks, as, in justice to the other students, the examiner must not give the "benefit of the doubt" in a case where slovenliness obliterates the feminine or the plural word-terminations which are asked.

I will say again what I have said many a time before. The cleverest papers, the papers which get most marks, are the most orderly and freest from blots.

I mean the preceding remarks to apply to my impressions on the results of the examination for both boys and girls, on each point mentioned. To the above remarks I add the following:—

The more even work, and perhaps, I may say, the more steady and careful preparation, is found among the girls' papers; on the other hand, the best papers—some of rare excellence—belong to the boys.

The average girls' papers were not very excellent: still they indicated that praiseworthy efforts had been made to deserve credit and a pass.

The average boys' papers were with very few exceptions absolutely bad, and gave no indication that they had prepared themselves with any intention of being successful.

On the whole more carelessness was observable in the boys' papers, especially in the average portion, than in the girls'. It is the duty of the Examiner to point out the failings both in the matter and the method of working; but the Examiner relishes and keeps for a long time the very high satisfaction left in his mind by the very fine result of a great many papers.

Junior Grade.—Boys.

Report of Albert Barrère, A. Courby, and E. Janau.

The work of the boys who took the French Paper for the Junior Grade shows a marked improvement on that sent in in previous years, and we are glad to report that the often repeated complaints about untidiness and want of order have been attended to. There are still, however, some schools where apparently the pupils are not trained to answer examination papers, and in several cases answers to grammatical questions were again found in fragments scattered among other matter, all this to the detriment of the candidate.

Several candidates do not seem to have realised the importance of the grammar questions. Their translation was good and they must have known enough grammar to pass, but by their careless treatment of it they failed to obtain the necessary marks.

The grammar questions were, however, answered satisfactorily on the whole. In question 1* the masculine of "tante" and "celle" proved to be stumbling blocks, as were also the feminine of "berger" and "duc." In question 2 few could give the singular of "beaux" or "eux." It was surprising to find how few knew "avoir" and "être," even among those who answered the rest of question 3 correctly; with regard to "ce," "cela," "celui," and "celui-là," question 5 (b.),† we found evidence of good teaching coupled with great confusion in the minds of the pupils. This is a point we must once more recommend to the attention of the teachers so that "celui" and "cela" may not be given again (e.g. cela plume, celui livre). Question 6‡ showed that many do not know that adverbs of quantity are followed by "de."

---

* "1. Give, in columns, the feminine of *berger*, *bref*, *acteur*, *majeur*, *duc*, [illegible], [illegible], [illegible]; and the masculine of *gentille*, *tante*, *celle*, *vieille*, *sa petite fille*, and their respective meaning.

"2. Give, in columns, the plural of [illegible], *cette croix*, *mon travail*, *du cheval*, *un caillou*, *un petit clou*, *son ail bleu*, and the singular of *victorieux*, *beaux*, *messieurs*, [illegible], *eux*.

"3. State the rule for the formation of ordinal numbers, and translate into French: Were they not eighty? He was the first and I was the seventh; the fifth, the ninth, and the thirty-first; number two hundred; it was a quarter to one; eight is the third of twenty-four."

† "5. (a.) Distinguish between the following words: *mais*, *mets*; [illegible]; *fol*, *fols*; [illegible]; *lieu*, *lieue*.

"(b.) Distinguish between *ce*, *cela*, *celui*, *celui-là*. Compose and translate short French sentences to illustrate the rules you give."

‡ "6. Translate into French: We have gathered many apples. She has less courage than her sister. Louisa is taller than her brother. How many books hast thou, John? You have little courage. Why do you make so much noise?"

The composition was attempted by a greater number than formerly, and on the whole showed thought and good teaching; some papers were very good.

The translation from the prepared books was satisfactory, but showed great differences in the care with which the work had been done. Apparently, in some cases, the translation is dictated and learnt by heart. But this dictation not being revised by the teachers the most ludicrous mistakes are made. In this way "vice" becomes "voice" and "huiles purifiées" appears in the disguise of "petrified holes."

Many did not know what was meant by parallel columns in D. (a) and gave an interlinear translation.

The unseen translation was satisfactory, considering the fact that it was somewhat more difficult than in the past.

JUNIOR GRADE.—GIRLS.

Report of JAMES BOÏELLE, B.A.

The general impression made upon me by the examination of the girls in the Junior Grade is a most favourable one, the general results pointing, in a very large number of papers, to a high standard of efficiency. Looking back some ten years ago upon a similar examination with which the Board was good enough to entrust me, there is no doubt that the general standard of work has considerably improved.

(1.) *Grammar.*—This was on the whole well done, in many cases excellently well. Question 5* was the least satisfactory. The relative values of *ce*, *cela*, *celui*, *celui-là* were not, as a rule, understood or explained. Question 4† (the verb question) while being in its more difficult and intricate part, viz., the irregular verbs, very successfully answered as a rule, was in its more elementary portion very poorly done; many, even among the most successful candidates, being unable to conjugate the present subjunctive of *être* and *avoir*.

(2.) *Prepared Books.*—This, on the whole, was very well done, showing that great care had been bestowed on the preparation. The first piece of Lamartine's Bernard de Palissy showed the greatest number of failures.

(3.) *Translation at sight.*—Considering the comparative difficulty of the piece set, it was in a large number of cases very successfully mastered; in some of the best papers, and they were not a few, almost faultlessly so. Two or three words, especially *paysannes*, *enfants aux yeux rouges*, and *étoffes* proved stumbling blocks. Want of care led the larger number of candidates to translate *paysannes* by peasants, instead of peasant *girls* or *women*, whilst in hundreds of instances, for reasons unknown to your examiner, *étoffes* was translated by *toffees*.

(4.) *Composition.*—This, of course the hardest part of the examination, was in the case of a large number of the best candidates most successfully attempted, and, as a whole, pleased me greatly. The

---

* "5. (a.) Distinguish between the following words: *mais*, *maïs*; *dessin*, *dessein*; *foi*, *fois*; *jeûner*, *jouir*; *lieu*, *lieue*.

(b.) Distinguish between *ce*, *cela*, *celui*, *celui-là*. Compose and translate short French sentences to illustrate the rules you give."

† "4. Write, in columns, (a.) the third person singular and the first person plural of the indicative present of *acheter*, *avancer*, *connaître*, *craindre*, *tirer*; (b.) the third person plural of the future, and the past participle of *cueillir*, *couvrir*, *prendre*, *pouvoir*, *courir*; and (c.) the subjunctive present, in full, of *avoir* and *être*."

first part, the detached sentences, was much better done than the second part, many who had successfully got through those breaking down completely in the continuous prose of the second part.

In conclusion, I should like to say that, taken as a whole, the examination is one in which the scholars, teachers, and the Board are to be congratulated.

PREPARATORY GRADE.—BOYS.

Report of LYDIE DECOUDUN and Rev. J. F. HOGAN.

The papers of the Preparatory Grade (Boys) examined by us this year were, on the whole, satisfactory, if we take into consideration the age of the candidates. The questions in grammar and in translation, prepared and unseen, were well answered by a large number of candidates. As usual, the chief defect was to be found in the composition, or translation of English into French. The examiners took great pains to provide a passage as easy and simple as possible for this portion of the programme, yet many of the candidates passed it by altogether, or made very poor attempts at answering it. Seeing that a large number of marks are allotted to this branch of the subject, both teachers and boys will find it to their interest to devote more attention to it in future.

PREPARATORY GRADE.—GIRLS.

Report of F. J. AMOURS and A. COCHET.

The Girls' papers are of a fair average quality and call for no special mention.

The answers to the grammatical questions on nouns, adjectives, numerals and verbs, show good drilling, even in cases where the rest of the paper is weak; the sections dealing with phrases are less satisfactory. The composition has been done very well by about twelve per cent. of the candidates; many others have struggled bravely through it, but one can hardly expect higher results in the translation of a connected piece at so early a stage when pupils have not yet had time to acquire an extensive vocabulary. The passages from Lamartine and Florian are well done, especially the poetry, which was the more difficult. The translation at sight is, on the whole, the most successful part of the paper.

COMMERCIAL FRENCH.

SENIOR GRADE.

Report of F. J. AMOURS.

The senior paper is decidedly the best of the three grades. The boys have only eight failures out of forty-two, and the girls none at all. The successful candidates have acquired a large stock of French and English technical terms and phrases which they use intelligently.

MIDDLE GRADE.

Report of F. J. AMOURS.

The Commercial Middle Grade shows a marked improvement on last year, not only in the percentages of honours and passes, but in the general tone of the papers. The absolute failures are not so frequent, and there is a more genuine commercial ring in the phraseology. The translation of English into French still leaves much to be desired.

JUNIOR GRADE.

Report of F. J. AMOURS.

It may be broadly stated that out of the 441 boys who went in for the Junior Commercial Paper 200 knew something of the subject (some not very much), and the rest nothing at all. The translations of the 'failures' are sometimes very funny reading; but such fun quickly palls on the examiner, who is ever asking himself on what grounds teachers or managers of schools could allow so many of their pupils to enter for an examination for which they were so evidently unfit. The time, however limited, that was devoted to the acquirement of a few commercial terms, would have been more usefully employed in improving the spelling and handwriting of the candidates, both being unusually bad. There is some very good work among the 17 per cent. that have obtained honours.

Owing to less self-confidence or to better guidance, only twenty-four girls presented papers; they have made a more creditable appearance, and only eight failed to reach pass marks.

GERMAN.

SENIOR, MIDDLE, JUNIOR, AND PREPARATORY.—BOYS AND GIRLS.

Report of ALBERT M. SELSS, LL.D.

In reading the 1,119 answer-books submitted to me for examination, I was, before all, agreeably struck with the steady increase in the number of the candidates in German. This number is now more than double that which it was some eight years ago, when I had for the last time the honour of examining in German.

I cannot say that the quality of the candidates has improved in the same ratio as the quantity.

It is true that cases of failure are, in the main, restricted to the two lower Grades, the Preparatory and the Junior; but in both they are numerous. The cause in nearly every instance is the same—imperfect answering in composition. Though tolerably able to make out, or else to guess, the meaning of a passage from the German, young candidates are often wholly at a loss to comprehend the rules for the order of words in a German sentence. They are also unacquainted with the genders of the nouns; they have no idea of the right endings of adjectives, and they do not know how to form the plural of substantives.

These defects are common to all beginners in German; but an imperfection which disfigures the answering of all the candidates—the Senior and the Middle Grade, as well as that of the Preparatory and the Junior, and which is peculiar to candidates for German in the classes for Intermediate education in Ireland—is the almost total disregard of the German dotted vowels.

Nearly all the candidates ignore the German *umlauts*. For an *ä* they put *a*; for an *ö* they write *o*, and similarly *u* for *ü*. Thus, the verb *wünschen*, to wish, in the 1,119 answer-books consistently is spelt *wunschen*, or else *wunchen*, the letter *s* having been dropped along with the umlaut over the letter *u*. This, and other similar imperfections, are due to the indifference of candidates to the sound and pronunciation of words, and is partly brought about by the absence of oral tests, and the pen-and-ink examination-system, in which the pronunciation of the foreign language counts for nothing.

Girls compared to Boys.—My attention has been carefully employed in comparing the success of the boys with that of the girls in respect of German.

In my opinion, any distinction between the two sexes in point of ability can never be very decided. There is no very palpable difference between boys and girls, as regards skill or talent for languages in general. The same course of instruction will do for both, and will, in a given time, produce much the same result with either of the two sexes—their cleverness being much the same.

However, a close scrutiny of the answer-books, when combined with observation of the different characters of boys and girls, might lead to the following distinctions:—

First.—Girls are the more painstaking; they prepare their work better; they have read the text-books more carefully—they toil harder for success. But, on the other hand, their intelligence is more apt to wander; they oftener miss the point of the question they are asked; their grammatical notions are less clear, and, in the long run, given equal amount of diligence, they will not be equal to the boys in point of success at German.

Second.—A decided source of weakness found in the answering of most girls, and a defect which confirms what I have said before, is their difficulty in distinguishing between subject and object, and in applying the several rules on the agreement between nouns, adjectives, participles, and certain other portions of the verb. Thus, five girls out of ten will put the accusative case after *sein*, *scheinen*, *bleiben* (to be, to seem, to remain), while only one boy out of ten will make the same mistake. This arises in part from the advantage which boys have over girls in learning Latin; for the ancient classical languages are the best training-ground for teaching and learning German as well.

Commercial German is up to the present anything but a success. The candidates are few; the answering is imperfect. Still this new department is one so eminently useful, and so important for the success of the whole scheme of Intermediate Education, that it would be better to lower the demands, and make the questions still fewer and still easier than they are, than to abandon them altogether. I cannot help confessing that the intricacies of commercial German are apt to terrify and dishearten candidates as yet imperfectly acquainted with ordinary German.

ITALIAN.

Senior Grade.—Boys and Girls.

Report of W. H. Murphy, D.D.

A clear and ready knowledge of Italian grammar was shown by the answering of questions on the accidence, but outside this limit the result was not so satisfactory. Thus, very few could indicate the distinction between open and closed vowel sounds, and fewer still could state what is meant by hiatus.

Acquaintance with Italian idioms, especially with the use of the conjunctive pronouns in their more complex combinations, was a gratifying feature in the answering of a large number of students, both boys and girls.

In reference to the prescribed books I have to remark—and this observation applies also to the Junior Grade—that while a very good knowledge was commonly possessed of the matter of the book, the attention of the students did not seem to have been drawn to the position held, whether by the author or the particular work, in reference to Italian Literature generally. Thus, in the Junior Grade, very few could name the kind of composition primarily associated with Metastasio, while in the Senior Grade equally few could explain in what respect the Merope was a protest against the dominant taste of the time.

The translation at sight was in agreeable contrast with the crude work of the students of the lower Grades.

Middle Grade.—Boys and Girls.

Report of W. H. Murphy, D.D.

A gratifying feature in the answering of a very large number of students, both boys and girls, was their acquaintance with Italian idioms, for example, with the uses of the subjunctive mood.

I have to remark, however, that students of this Grade were quite unprepared for questions of history and geography arising out of the text of the prescribed authors—questions the admissibility of which is explicitly laid down in Notes on the Programme, Note 2. Thus, not a solitary student had ever heard of the Countess Matilda, and several referred to the Adige as a river of Egypt. One student observed that as she had been unable to find an annotated copy of Tasso, she thought it unfair that such questions should be asked! The suggestion conveyed to teachers by this observation needs no additional point.

Little praise can be given to the translation at sight in this Grade. A word for word version was always produced, but seldom an intelligible statement.

Junior Grade.—Boys and Girls.

Report of W. H. Murphy, D.D.

Beyond the general statement that the answering was largely good, the papers examined suggest but two remarks:—First, that, as regards composition, there is a near approach to equality between boys and girls, although the boys have a slight advantage. Secondly, that a minute and intelligent acquaintance with the prescribed poetical work, taken as a whole, seems to have been very generally imparted.

The unfavourable comment passed on the translation at sight in the preparatory paper applies in terms to a very large number of junior students.

Preparatory Grade.—Boys and Girls.

Report of W. H. Murphy, D.D.

The answering all round was good, but no paper viewed as a whole was of superior merit.

The grammar questions were commonly well answered, except Questions 5 and 6*. Many students did not know what was required of them when they were asked to write an augmentative and a diminutive in combination with a given word, and a very large number failed to write the cardinal numbers correctly.

The composition, which was in the main an easy exercise on the conjunctive pronouns, showed that this difficult feature had been well mastered by a large proportion of students. The superiority of the boys over the girls was marked. The highest marking in the case of a boy was 92 per cent. of the total assigned to composition (several ranging from 84 to 90 per cent.), while the highest percentage obtained by a girl was 60, and only two attained to this.

The weak point in the answering, both of boys and girls, was the translation at sight, especially the continuous sentences. Very few indeed seemed to realise that the passage when done into English should make sense.

Commercial, Senior, Middle, and Junior Grades.—Boys and Girls.

Report of Rev. W. H. Murphy, D.D.

There were in all but six candidates. They all had a good knowledge of Italian in reference to their respective Grades, and this enabled them to answer fairly. Little evidence, however, of special training was displayed, and a vocabulary poor in technical phrases was common to all the candidates.

CELTIC.

Senior Grade.—Boys.

Report of T. J. Flannery.

Twenty-six Senior students took "Celtic" this year—all boys. The number is not large, but the character of the work done by them was very solid, and therefore very gratifying. There were but very few failures, and over half the students passed with honours.

The paper was not by any means a too easy one, yet on the whole it was faced and answered very manfully. Many of the candidates made the highest possible marks on several of the questions, showing how

---

* "5. Give two examples of augmentatives, two of diminutives, and write the word [illegible] and [illegible] in combination with the examples.

"6. Write the cardinal numbers from ten to twenty."

well prepared they were for their work. Not only the pieces from the prescribed authors, but also the "unseen" extracts were generally well translated.

In this, as well as in other Grades, however, students will sometimes —owing to haste or to want of experience—entirely mistake a question and write something which may be very correct and very admirable, but which is valueless for the purpose of the examination, because it was not really asked for. Periodical examinations and careful correction of the students' papers would tend to prevent this.

The answers to the second grammar question—"What traces are there in modern Irish of a *neuter gender*? Of a *dual number*? Of *deponent verbs*?"—were very disappointing. Few students touched the question at all, and those who did answered it in the most fragmentary and unsatisfactory manner. Yet an examiner might fairly expect Senior students—youths old enough to matriculate at a university—to have gone at least thus far out of the well-worn beaten track, and to have an intelligent notion of some at least of the phenomena that strike one in Irish at every turn.

In all the Grades one notices a great want of accuracy in writing proper names. Naturally this want of accuracy is more noticeable in the papers of the Junior candidates, but in them it is more excusable. One would like to see, however, more accuracy in this respect amongst Middle and Senior students. Queen Meadhbh, for instance, had her name spelt twenty different ways amongst as many students, though the form just given is absolutely the only admissible one in modern Irish. If the ancient form *Medb* were consistently adhered to, it would be tolerable, but it was not. In the phrase *go haimsir Chuire* (Keating) not one student in ten saw that *Chuire* here was the genitive of *Core*, and that this latter was the only correct form in an English translation. The phrase, however, was generally translated "to the time of Cuire," some even writing "to the time of Chuire." Such errors are due to carelessness and want of accurate observation, and teachers are strongly advised to give more attention to this subject, as it is of more importance than many of them think.

MIDDLE GRADE.—BOYS.

Report of T. J. FLANNERY.

The numbers entered for the two upper Grades—Middle and Senior—were, as might be expected, much less than those entered for the lower Grades. Only forty-six students took the Middle Grade Celtic, but the comparative results are higher than in any other Grade, for there is a smaller proportion of failures with the highest proportion of honours—these numbering more than a half of the whole. We should hope therefore that such successes would induce a much larger number of students to compete in this Grade next year.

In this Grade the candidates begin to show a more exact and more thorough knowledge of Irish Grammar. The "sight" pieces were translated remarkably well throughout; the composition was well attempted in most cases, and the Irish phrases were in general sensibly and accurately translated, giving evidence of careful and accurate teaching. It is a pleasure to see that Middle Grade students have got over the silliness of translating phrases word for word, and have some conception of the meaning of *idiom*.

The weak points were the grammatical analysis, and the identification of the place-names. Though only two short lines were given for analysis, few students attempted the question at all, and of those who did, some had but a very hazy notion of what was wanted. Only a very small number had any clear idea of the *meaning* of the two lines—failing which, of course it was hopeless to look for any clear explanation of the relation of the parts.

One would expect Irish students to know the famous places of their own country, more especially the few that are referred to in the texts they have studied; and one would think it should be a pleasure to them to identify those places under their various names, and to connect the native names with the anglicised ones. But even the few mentioned in the prescribed works were very indifferently or not at all known—with some candidates the places were all in Scotland, others had no difficulty in locating them all in Mayo, whilst others again found situations for them all in the County Kerry.

Junior Grade.—Boys.

Report of T. J. Flannery.

In the Junior Grade of Celtic 307 students presented themselves for examination—nearly as many as there were in the Preparatory Grade, and the results were still more gratifying, for there were fewer failures and a much larger number of honours.

The set pieces were as a rule well done. It is always a question whether word-for-word translation is a proof of real knowledge or only a cloak for ignorance, but whilst in a few cases a very fair literal translation was given with obviously very little idea of the general meaning, still a much larger number shirked the word-for-word translation, finding it probably too exacting, and satisfied themselves with a rough and very free translation of the piece as a whole, omitting the Irish text. Whilst the composition was in general very creditable, many gave no evidence that they had ever tried to form—or been asked to form—an Irish sentence even of the shortest.

Many students in this and other Grades appear to spend themselves in *penmanship* to the neglect of more useful and more solid acquirements. Teachers would do well to direct their pupils' attention to such important points as grammar, spelling, and composition, rather than mere penmanship, which, however admirable, is not by any means the be-all and end-all of Irish scholarship. And at least if the Irish character be used, a cursive hand—such as many have acquired to perfection—should be cultivated; for in writing each character separately, as a few candidates have unwisely tried to do, the subject matter is apt to be forgotten or neglected, not to speak of the great loss of time involved in such laboured writing. Occasionally indeed a student's subject matter will be quite equal to his elegant handwriting, tempting one almost to the conclusion that he who is good at one thing will be good all round, but the too frequent recurrence of fine penmanship with little or no exact knowledge shows what a hasty and false conclusion it is.

Here, as in the Preparatory Grade, parsing is still too much in the English style, "neuter genders," "present participles," and other things quite foreign to Irish grammar being frequently spoken of, whilst the real Irish peculiarities are unnoticed.

Preparatory Grade.—Boys.

Report of T. J. Flannery.

The results of the examination in Celtic this year are generally very encouraging. Naturally the two lower Grades were the most largely represented, 312 students presenting themselves in the Preparatory, and 307 in the Junior Grade. In the Preparatory Grade nearly three-fourths of the whole passed, considerably more than a third of all the passes being in Honours.

The pieces from the prescribed author were generally well translated, in some cases very well indeed. The real test, however, of the knowledge of a language—as far as a written paper can show it—lies in the power to translate at sight, and in the ability to manage the composition exercises, the latter especially. Considering the age of the Preparatory Grade students a very praiseworthy attempt was made to deal with the "at sight" pieces. Among the curiosities of answering here is to be noticed the general difficulty in identifying the *Sionnach*. Hundreds of students—Preparatory and Junior—failed to make him out, and the whole animal kingdom was searched in the effort to identify him; with some he was a bear, with others a bullock, whilst others again made him out a frog, or a spider. One would not have expected so well-known and distinctive an Irish name for a *fox* to present such a difficulty.

The composition exercise was naturally the hardest, though the phrases given in this (Preparatory) Grade were very short and simple. Here most of the failures occurred, though on the other hand many of the candidates showed a very creditable command of Irish idiom. The parsing for the most part was too much after the English model, few of the students realising that the Irish language has phenomena of its own. So little was this fact present to the minds of some boys that they actually translated the Irish sentence into English and then parsed the English sentence—for which of course no marks could be given. It was surprising too how many seemed ignorant of the native name of the language in which they were being examined, when asked to turn into Gaelic the phrase "He speaks Irish very well." Over and over again the Examiner found "Celtic" and "Irish" and even "Erinn" given as equivalents for the word "Irish" in that sentence—all written, too, in most unexceptionable Irish penmanship. It would be difficult to believe the same boys could have learned as much French without knowing the French name of that language.

Girls.—All Grades.

Of the 891 students who took up "Celtic" this year only five were girls—three being in the Preparatory Grade, one in the Junior, and one in the Middle. The smallness of this number is much to be wondered at, and much to be regretted. There seems no good reason why, when so very considerable a number of boys from all parts of the country take up this subject, so extremely few of their sisters and cousins should interest themselves in this peculiarly Irish and national study. Certainly they have no reason to be afraid of the subject, nor of the competition of the boys, for examined in the very same papers as were given to the Boys—there were no special Girls' Papers in the subject this year—they have proved themselves at least their equals, there was no failure, all five passed in honours—one of the five attaining one of the very highest places, and proving that, in some cases at least, excellent matter may be found combined with beautiful penmanship. One of the causes why so few girls enter for "Celtic" is perhaps the scarcity of qualified women teachers. But it should be as easy now for women to qualify themselves as teachers of Irish as it is for men. It is to be hoped that the marked success of the few girls who have taken it up this year will encourage many more to take it up next year and not leave this valuable accomplishment and all the honours to their brothers.

SPANISH.

Junior, Middle, and Senior Grades.

Report of V. Steinberger, M.A.

The answering in Spanish in the Junior, Middle, and Senior Grades was, with the exception of two candidates, unsatisfactory. The grammar alone seems to have been attended to by the majority of students, and to this circumstance they owe their pass marks; but even in this branch a large number of inaccuracies show a very imperfect preparation.

There was almost a general weakness in translation of the passages taken from the prescribed authors, as the sense was missed in many instances. The text books seem either not to have been read at all, or only very cursorily.

The translation at sight was equally poor.

The impression left on my mind after the correction of the papers was that the study of Spanish seems to be carried on largely by private study, and in a very superficial manner.

Of the two better candidates mentioned above, I remarked special excellence in a Senior Grade candidate.

DOMESTIC ECONOMY.

(Girls only).

Senior Grade.

Report of Elizabeth Moore.

In most cases the answering in the Senior Grade was fairly good, and in not a few cases it was excellent.

The part of the subject which seemed to have got least attention was the section on cookery. I was surprised how few girls knew exactly how to prepare and boil a cabbage.

It would be well if the students could get a little experience at home in the simple matters connected with household management, as in school there is not time to spare for showing girls how to cook, wash, dust rooms, &c., &c., and when we consider that these are matters on which, more or less, the comfort of all households depends, surely it is worth while for girls to study carefully the whole subject.

The chief fault in the method of answering was a want of conciseness.

The candidates seemed to think that the longer the answer the better; in some cases pages and pages were written which could well have been omitted.

At the same time anyone reading the Senior Grade papers could see that the text books had, in most cases, been carefully taught and studied.

Middle Grade.

Report of Mary Bellingham Todd.

In this Grade the papers were uniformly good though a little mechanical where the questions could be answered by "the book." More satisfactory were the answers to Questions Nos. 1, 2, and 5,* in these instances the work was performed on broader lines, less of book-work was evident, but a thorough grasp of the subject was shown in the intelligent illustrations appended by many of the students. In some few cases, however, the inability to keep to the question was strongly marked, and where a description of the *pulmonary* circulation was required, the answer was imbedded in a complete account of the *greater* and *portal* circulations.

To the question on the *nitrogenous* elements, very few correct answers were given, instead a number of *compounds* were tabulated.

Cookery, an art which ought to have a special attraction for girls, receives but scant attention at their hands judging from the answers to Question No. 10; † the most elementary knowledge of the subject would prevent the confusion of the terms *boiling* and *stewing*.

Junior Grade.

Report of Elizabeth Moore and Mary Bellingham Todd.

The answers in this Grade were on the whole good, and in a few cases exceedingly so.

It would be well if girls had impressed upon them the advisability of answering the questions asked without introducing matters foreign to the subject, *e.g.*, in question No. 9‡ a goodly number of the answers included directions for every possible method of cooking. No. 7,§ however, elicited a praiseworthy amount of practical knowledge, with but few unnecessary statements.

Although it would be impossible to give much time during Domestic Economy lessons to such subjects as "How to boil a cabbage," or "How to prepare a lather for washing woollen articles," yet by a little judicious questioning and encouragement girls might be induced to take a livelier interest in these practical home matters.

We are pleased to add that many of the papers were carefully written and arranged.

---

* "1. What change takes place in the air of a room where gas is burning? On what does the light of a flame depend? By what simple plan would you prevent the air of a room becoming exhausted without causing a draught?

"2. Describe the structure of the skin. What is perspiration? Name its chief functions.

"5. Write a short note on the pulmonary circulation. Describe clearly the change that takes place in the blood during this circulation."

† "10. What ingredients would you add to 2 lbs. of coarse beef in making a savoury stew? Of what material should the stew-pot be made? What degree of heat should be allowed in the process?"

‡ "9. How many kinds of frying are there? Which do you recommend, and why?"

§ "7. Describe exactly how to light a fire. How is the air of a room affected by a fire in the grate?"

ELEMENTARY MECHANICS.

Senior Grade.—Boys only.

Report of Rev. F. Lennon, D.D.

A fair proportion of boys have shown a good knowledge of Elementary Mechanics; and although no one has succeeded in obtaining full marks, there are some whose acquaintance with the subject extends even beyond the limits of the programme. In a very large number of cases, however, vagueness of conception, want of precision in expression, and a tendency to rely on memory rather than reasoning power in the application of formulæ are conspicuous.

PLANE TRIGONOMETRY.

Senior Grade.

Report of John R. Leebody, M.A., D.Sc.

Boys of the Prescribed Age.

The result of the examination was satisfactory, as more than two-thirds of those examined passed. The answering of the successful competitors was on the whole good, and in some cases very good, one candidate obtaining full marks, and several others almost full marks. A considerable number of those who reached the honour standard had evidently been very well taught and familiarized with neat trigonometrical methods. Long, laborious, and inelegant methods of solution were clearly the limit of the experience of others. A weak point with many of the candidates indicated defective algebraical rather than trigonometrical knowledge; this was their inability to deal satisfactorily with any problem involving the simplification of surds. If, in the solution of a trigonometrical problem, the necessity of expressing a fraction containing surds as a decimal should arise, it should not be an insuperable barrier to further progress.

Boys (over-age).

The number of competitors was not large, and the statistics in regard to them will best explain their status. Twenty-four candidates presented themselves for examination; 6 of these passed with honours, 3 passed, and 15 failed. Two of the honour candidates made very fine answers, one obtaining full marks and the other obtaining ninety-two per cent.

Girls.

There were very few (only 11) competitors; of these 8 passed, 2 reaching the honour standard, and 3 failed. The subject clearly does not receive much attention in our girls' schools.

ALGEBRA AND ARITHMETIC.

Senior Grade.

Report of A. E. Lyster, M.A.

Boys.

The Senior Grade answering in Algebra and Arithmetic was in very many cases highly creditable. In Arithmetic some of the candidates did much extra work from failing to consider what was wanted, and how their work might be simplified.

The average knowledge exhibited of Series, Permutations, Binomial Theorem, and the translation of problems into Algebraic symbols was distinctly satisfactory. The solutions of the quadratic equations in two unknowns were not so encouraging. The necessity of obtaining all the roots and of grouping them in corresponding pairs was not generally apprehended, and the calculations were frequently made cumbrous by a neglect of reducing numerical fractions to their lowest terms.

Girls.

The Senior Grade answering in Algebra and Arithmetic was in many cases creditable. In Arithmetic some of the candidates did much extra work from failing to consider what was wanted and how their work might be simplified.

The average knowledge exhibited of Series, Permutations, Binomial Theorem, and the translation of problems into Algebraic symbols was satisfactory. The solutions of the quadratic equations in two unknowns were not so encouraging. The necessity of obtaining all the roots and of grouping them in corresponding pairs was not generally apprehended, and the calculations were sometimes made cumbrous by a neglect of reducing numerical fractions to their lowest terms. Some of the candidates might have obtained higher marks by confining their attention to a part of the course and mastering it thoroughly before proceeding further.

EUCLID.

Senior Grade.—Boys.

Report of J. J. Alexander, M.A.

The paper set consisted of eleven questions, 1-7 being propositions, and 8-11 deductions.

The propositions were very creditably worked by most of the candidates. The statements and conclusions were often omitted or badly expressed, but the rest of the work was generally fairly correct. Several slips were made in writing down proportions, and more care should be taken in distinguishing a "third" from a "mean proportional." Many candidates, strange to say, invoked the aid of the converse to III. 22 to prove that the four angles of a quadrilateral make four right angles, instead of using I. 32, Cor.

The deductions were not very often done except 9,* which gave rise to many creditable solutions.

As in the Middle Grade, the chief faults were:—

(1.) Excessive abbreviation.
(2.) Faulty drawing.
(3.) Neglect to number answers.
(4.) Overcrowding.
(5.) Use of the official margin.

These faults were not so marked in this Grade as in the Middle.

There seemed to be a large preponderance of intelligent and careful, if not brilliant, candidates in this examination.

Senior Grade.—Girls.

Report of Charles Smith, M.A.

In the examination in Euclid of Senior Grade Girls there is little matter for comment except the general uniformity of the answering exhibited by the candidates. Of the 47 candidates whose papers were sent to me only 5 failed to get the 125 marks necessary to pass the examination, while the marks obtained by the others vary, with few exceptions, between 190 and 240 out of a possible 500. The examination paper set contained 11 questions, of which 7 were propositions from Euclid and 4 were riders. The answering to the book questions was in general accurate and complete, but very few of the candidates made any attempt at the riders. None attempted more than one rider, and of those who did only two succeeded in obtaining a correct solution. In a few other cases I gave partial credit for attempts that showed a knowledge of the principles of geometrical analysis, even though the correct solution was not obtained.

In question 6 on the paper the first part (vi. 15) was answered correctly by nearly all the candidates, but most of them omitted the second part—to define reciprocally proportional. Some of those who did attempt the definition seemed to have little idea of its meaning, although they had correctly proved the property for the sides of equal triangles having an angle in one equal to an angle in the other. The same was noticeable in the answering of the Junior Grade Boys who were asked to define a rectilineal angle. In both cases the proposition that formed the main part of the question seemed to have been committed to memory by many candidates without their having a clear idea of the meaning of the terms involved.

The answering to the questions set from the first four books of Euclid was in general accurate and calls for no comment.

Middle Grade.—Boys.

Report of J. J. Alexander, M.A.

The paper set consisted of twelve questions, 1–8 being propositions and 9–12 deductions.

The propositions were, on the whole, well done, except by the Over-age candidates. Question 3,† in which the Euclid enunciation was disguised,

---

* "9. From a point A outside a given circle draw a straight line ABC cutting the circle in B and C, so that AB = BC."

† "3. State and prove a proposition of Euclid from which it is an immediate inference that the difference of the squares on two right lines is equal to a rectangle of which the sides are respectively equal to the sum of the lines and their difference."

caused most failures. It is clear from this that many students trusted to their memories rather than to their reasoning powers. Teachers would do well to frequently bring possible disguises of propositions, especially those needed in more advanced work, under the notice of their pupils.

The deductions were frequently attempted, often successfully. The close resemblance in enunciation of 9* to Book II., Prop. 11, deceived some and aided others, but no one seems to have thought of an equilateral triangle inscribed in a square with one vertex at a corner.

The chief faults were :—

(1.) *Excessive abbreviation.* Candidates were permitted to use all *intelligible* abbreviations; but an abbreviation, to be intelligible, should clearly convey (*a*) the meaning intended, and (*b*) no other possible meaning. For example, "⊙" sometimes stood for "circle," and sometimes for "centre"; "<" sometimes for "angle," sometimes for "rightangle," sometimes for "less than," and sometimes for the 12th letter of the alphabet; " = " sometimes for "is (or "are") "equal to" (the generally accepted equivalent), sometimes for the adjective "equal," and sometimes for "parallel." Other instances might be given, all tending to show that, in the interests of good and careful work, the habit of abbreviating should be restrained rather than encouraged.

(2.) *Faulty Drawing.* Many of the figures sent in were very inaccurate and slovenly, as when a circle was shown with its centre almost on the circumference, &c. It would benefit students, not only in Euclid, but in many other subjects, if their teachers insisted on their taking a reasonable amount of trouble to get correct diagrams. It would be well also if the convention of denoting points in Euclid by *printed capitals* were more generally observed. Some put *capitals* in the *figures* and *small letters* in the proofs.

(3.) Neglect to number answers. This was a common fault, and its frequency is surprising. Some omitted to number any of their answers, while others attached wrong numbers.

(4.) *Overcrowding.* This could be avoided by making each fresh step begin a new line on the paper, and by leaving a clear space abreast of the diagram.

(5.) A few of the examinees used the official margin of the answer books for their marginal references throughout. This is contrary to the Instructions, and such students would have been wiser to have provided themselves with an inner column for such references.

Middle Grade.—Girls.

Report of James J. Gibney, M.A.

The answering in this examination, judged from a pass standard, was very satisfactory. Few of the students failed to show a good knowledge of Euclid's propositions, and some were very exact indeed in giving the steps of their proofs and in quoting the authorities that they appealed to. It was however somewhat disappointing to find that many who knew the book-work accurately were unable to make even the slightest attempt at the solution of a deduction.

* "9. Divide a straight line into two parts such that the square on the whole line together with the square on one part shall be equal to twice the square on the other part."

JUNIOR GRADE—BOYS OF THE PRESCRIBED AGE.

Report of JAMES J. GIBNEY, M.A., A. W. PANTON, M.A., SC.D., and CHARLES SMITH, M.A.

The answering of the candidates was about up to the average of former years, and does not appear to call for any special observation.

Although in many instances the answers were sent in with good diagrams and general neatness of style, we think there is on the whole great need for improvement in this respect. The figures were often very badly drawn, much too small, and crowded into the explanatory text, in such a way that the examiner had much difficulty in reading the answer.

The handwriting, also spelling, and punctuation were in many instances defective. We think it desirable that the attention of teachers should be directed to these faults, with a view to their correction in the future.

JUNIOR GRADE.—GIRLS.

Report of JOHN R. LEEBODY, M.A., D.SC.

GIRLS OF THE PRESCRIBED AGE.

The general result of the examination seems to me very satisfactory, as some 70 per cent. of those examined passed, and over 40 per cent of those who passed secured honours. The proportion of those passing with honours would have been considerably higher, had the candidates been better trained in the full and accurate statement of geometrical results. Marks had frequently to be deducted on account of omissions made in writing out constructions or demonstrations. Candidates are very properly permitted to abbreviate and condense their work, but the *omission of an essential point* in a demonstration, or *the failure to state* a construction is not, as some of them appear to imagine, an "*intelligible abbreviation.*" In the accurate statement of definitions even the best of the candidates seemed weak, the great majority of those examined failing to define accurately "a rectilineal angle." On the other hand I was pleased to see that a considerable number of them were able to deal with the Second Book propositions set (Prop. VII. and Prop. IX), without having recourse to the cumbrous and antiquated methods of Euclid's text. Reviewing the examinations as a whole I am able to say that the answering shows a marked improvement on what it was some ten years ago, and convinces me that Geometry is at present very well taught in a number of our girls' schools, and that these schools contain pupils with a decided aptitude for Mathematics.

GIRLS (OVER-AGE).

The number of candidates was not large, only twenty-four in all. Thirteen of these passed, most of them showing a fair knowledge of Euclid's text.

JUNIOR GRADE.—BOYS—OVER-AGE.

Report of JOHN R. LEEBODY, M.A., D.SC.

The majority of the candidates examined showed a very fair acquaintance with the text of Euclid, and more than two-thirds of them passed. The method of writing out propositions however was, in many cases, very prolix and old-fashioned. The impression left on my mind was that a good many of the candidates had been poorly taught in the beginning of their geometrical studies, and trained in methods much less modern than those which obtain in our best Intermediate Schools.

PREPARATORY GRADE.—BOYS.

Report of E. HUGHES DOWLING, B.A., and JOHN ENGLAND, M.A., D.SC.

The great majority of the candidates appear to have learned the propositions in the First and Second Books of Euclid fairly well—many very accurately. Comparatively few were able to solve the additional exercises, and most of the attempts were complete failures.

As always happens at such examinations some candidates were totally ignorant of the subject; some also had learned only the First Book, and exhibited no knowledge of the Second.

It may be useful to direct the attention of teachers to the inaccurate use of symbols, *e.g.*, the signs $>$ and $<$ are continually confounded; the word *bisect* is used to denote the division into any two parts; and worst of all the figure 2 is used to denote "to"; as for example, AB = 2 CD for AB = CD. Again, the statement that the two sides AB and BC of the one triangle are respectively equal to the two sides ED and DF of another is written

$$2\ AB + BC = 2\ ED + DF.$$

This is often followed by the too liberal use of "*and*" instead of "*therefore*," as, and the angle B = the angle D *and* the base AC = the base EF, *and* the triangle ABC = the triangle DEF. This we regard as the result of careless teaching, and should be particularly attended to, as it is a grave defect in a boy's mental training and logical reasoning powers. Another source of great inconvenience to examiners is the indiscriminate use of capital and small letters; the former in the figures and the latter, but not consistently, in the demonstration. From the failure to work the exercises it is evident that too little attention is given to this part of the subject, for pupils learn the propositions more easily if they are taught to make intelligent attempts at exercises, and the master loses less time in hearing the propositions.

PREPARATORY GRADE.—GIRLS.

Report of A. W. PANTON, M.A., D.SC.

Out of 222 candidates examined over 100 failed to pass, and of these thirty-nine obtained no marks at all. This result must be regarded as very unsatisfactory; for although no great knowledge of Geometry is to be looked for in girls so young as those who present themselves for examination in this Grade, yet it is to be presumed that only those are sent up in the subject who are supposed by their teachers to have some taste for the study of it, and to be fairly well prepared. Most of the candidates—most even of those who failed to pass—had evidently spent considerable time in the preparation of the two Books of Euclid appointed. It is worth the consideration of teachers whether this time might not have been more profitably spent in the study of some more congenial subject. In the answers to the propositions it was not difficult to find, in the case even of most of those who obtained honour marks, evidence of dependence on memory rather than an intelligent comprehension of Euclid's proof. The deducibles set were of a very elementary character, but few of the candidates showed any capacity for dealing with them. Attention may be called to one notable exception —that of a girl who answered all the deducibles in very good style, and failed by twenty marks only to secure the full total of 600. Most of those who attempt these exercises show an utter disregard of logic, making no scruple to assume anything, whether true or false, which may appear likely to lead to the desired solution.

It is satisfactory to be able to add a word in praise of the handwriting and general neatness with which the answers were in most instances sent in; and of the spelling, which contrasts most favourably with that of the boys of the Junior Grade examined by me.

ALGEBRA.

* Middle Grade—Boys.

Report of W. M'F. Orr, M.A.

The general standard of the answering of the Middle Grade Boys appears to have been neither very high nor very low compared with that attained in previous years. Two boys obtained 595 marks out of the 600.

The first question, as was to be expected, was done correctly by a very large proportion of the candidates; some did not arrange their work properly in powers of x, while in this as in other questions, when subtracting one expression from another containing a number of the same terms, the boys almost invariably cancelled such terms; this operation, besides making the work less legible, is quite unintelligible to any

---

* 1. Divide—

$$x^4+3(a-b)x^3-(3ab-2a^2-2b^2)x^2-3ab(a+b)x-2a^2b^2 \text{ by } x(x+2a)-b(x-3a).$$

2. Find the Highest Common Factor of—

$$bx(a^2x^2+b^2y^2)-ay(x^4+b^4) \text{ and}$$
$$by(a^2y^2+b^2x^2)-ax(y^4+b^4).$$

3. Find four consecutive numbers, such that the sum of the reciprocals of the first and fourth shall be equal to twice the reciprocal of the second.

4. Find the square root of the cube of the expression—

$$a^2x^2+2abx+b^2+2ac+\frac{2bc}{x}+\frac{c^2}{x^2}.$$

5. Divide $4x^{\frac{3}{2}}-\frac{1}{2}x^{-\frac{3}{2}}$ by $x^{\frac{1}{2}}-\frac{1}{2}x^{-\frac{1}{2}}$.

6. Solve the equation—

$$\sqrt[3]{x+3}+\sqrt[3]{x+2}=\sqrt[3]{5-2}.$$

7. Find x, y, and z, in their simplest forms, from the equations—

$$(a+b)x+(b+c)y+(c+a)z=0.$$
$$(a-b)x+(b-c)y+(c-a)z=0.$$
$$cx+ay+bz=a^3+b^3+c^3-3abc.$$

person reading it, unless care is taken to designate each pair of like terms by a mark peculiar to themselves, as was not done in a single instance. Very few succeeded in doing the second question, and nearly all those who did used the method of factors. Most of those who tried it by division failed, because they did not arrange the two expressions properly in powers of any one letter. In doing the fourth question some candidates merely extracted the square root of the expression given. Others left the answer in the form $\left(ax+b+\frac{c}{x}\right)^2$ while others again, in the expansion of this expression, made mistakes which a knowledge of the principle of symmetry should have rendered impossible. The idea that $x^{\frac{1}{2}} \times x^{-\frac{1}{2}} = x$ was the source of the most common mistake in the fifth question. The sixth question proved a great stumbling block, a great proportion of the candidates failing to present the equation correctly rationalized, while nearly all those who succeeded merely quoted the result. In doing the seventh question very few added and subtracted the first and second of the equations given, which would have considerably simplified the work. In this question also very bad mistakes were made in violation of the principle of symmetry. In the solutions of the seventh, eighth, tenth, eleventh, and twelfth questions there was to be noticed a general want of numerical accuracy that must be severely condemned. In the ninth question few succeeded in evaluating the radical that occurs in the solution. The solutions of this question to some extent, and those of the tenth still more, evidenced the fact that many of the candidates instead of knowing the rule for factorizing a quadratic expression by the same process as a quadratic equation should be solved, viz., completing the square, depend for the solution of the equation on *guessing* the factors of the corresponding expression. Many also in the case of these two questions did not solve the equations, but quoted, often wrongly, the formula for the result. In the eleventh and twelfth questions many of the boys did not lighten the numerical work, and diminish correspondingly the risk of error by reducing the equations obtained to their simplest forms before proceeding to their solution. Only in a few solitary instances did the candidates find both solutions of the twelfth question.

The answering of the over-age candidates was very bad; none obtained fifty per cent. of the total marks.

---

8. Solve the equations—

$$\frac{3x-y+5}{7}+\frac{5y-4z+3}{6}=\frac{4}{3}(2x-3),$$

$$\frac{3x-5y+16}{11}-\frac{2x-3y+6z}{13}=2y-z,$$

$$x-2y+z=0.$$

9. Solve the equation—

$$(1-a^2)(1-b^2)x^2-2(a+b)(1-ab)x+4ab=0.$$

10. Solve the equation—

$$\frac{x-4}{x+4}-\frac{x+4}{x-4}+\frac{804}{84}=0.$$

11. The fore wheel of a carriage makes 88 revolutions more than the hind wheel in going a mile, but if the circumference of the hind wheel be increased by 18 inches the fore wheel will make 120 revolutions more than the hind wheel in going a mile. Find the circumference of each wheel.

12. The amount of a sum of money and its simple interest for 5 years is £600. If the sum were £30 less and the rate of interest 1 per cent. more, the amount would be the same in 6½ years. Find the sum and the rate of interest.

* MIDDLE GRADE.—GIRLS.

Report of JAMES C. REA, B.A.

The answering of this Grade was satisfactory, more than half the candidates have passed, and a fair proportion of these have got honour marks. One of the honour candidates sent in an excellent paper. As to the questions in detail, I found that Questions 1, 5, and 10 were, in general, well done. Question 2 was worked by some of the candidates in the easiest manner by factorizing both expressions. Of those who tried the question in the ordinary way a great many made a hopeless muddle of it by not arranging each expression in powers of either x or y before division. The problems, *i.e.*, Questions 3, 11, and 12, were seldom done. This is the more surprising in the case of Question 3, as it is the easiest question on the paper. Some candidates made the silly mistake in Question 4 of cubing first and extracting the square root after, finding in almost every case that the labour of such a method was too great for them. Question 6 was not often attempted, and many took the sign of the cube root as indicating the third power. A small percentage of the candidates knew how to solve Question 7 in the proper manner, viz., by getting the ratios of x y and z from the first two equations. Great inaccuracy of work was displayed in attempts to solve Questions 8 and 9. It is a pity more attention is not given to accuracy when preparing for examinations. Many candidates who fail would pass if they were accurate in their work.

The answering of the over-age girls in this Grade was extremely bad, only two out of the seventeen candidates who presented themselves for the examination succeeded in getting pass marks.

---

† JUNIOR GRADE.—BOYS OF THE PRESCRIBED AGE.

Report of Rev. M. BARRETT, A. E. LYSTER, M.A., and JAMES C. REA, B.A.

The answering of the Junior Grade boys was in general fairly satisfactory. It may be well to direct the attention of teachers and pupils to the fact that several candidates suffered rather severely, and many failed to secure a pass owing to carelessness and great inaccuracy in their work; indeed, from the number of candidates who received practically no marks we must infer that many of them should not have been presented for the examination.

In the working of the questions we noticed a general neglect of the

---

* See note, pp. 33, 54.

[BOYS AND GIRLS.]

† 1. Simplify the expression—

$$\frac{1}{(x+1)(x+2)}+\frac{1}{(x+2)(x+3)}+\frac{1}{(x+3)(x+4)}.$$

2. Multiply together—

$$x+a+b,\ x+a-b,\ x-a+b,\ \text{and}\ x-a-b.$$

3. Simply the fraction—

$$\frac{(a-b)^3+(b+c)^3-(c+a)^3}{(a-b)(b+c)}.$$

4. Find the simplest form of the product of—

$$\frac{\dfrac{x^4+y^4}{x-y}-\dfrac{x^4-y^4}{x+y}}{\dfrac{x^2+y^2}{x-y}-\dfrac{x^2-y^2}{x+y}}\ \text{and}\ \left[\frac{1}{x^2-xy+y^2}+\frac{1}{x^2+xy+y^2}\right].$$

5. Reduce to its simplest form the fraction—

$$\frac{x^6+x^5-2x^4-x^3+3x^2-3x-6}{x^3-x^2-4x-2}.$$

use of brackets, and little power was shown of working questions in the simplest manner. This remark particularly applies to Questions 7, 8, and 10. The equations were badly done, and some candidates had no intelligent knowledge of what they were doing, as x and y very often appeared in the values of these quantities which they gave as answers. Questions 1, 4, and 5 were generally well done, but few did Questions 2 and 3 in the simplest way. Some candidates were able to factorise the expressions in Question 6, but could not write down the L.C.M. of those factors—this could hardly occur if they had a clear idea of what the L.C.M. meant. Many candidates tried to work Question 9 by clearing of fractions, and in doing so neglected to multiply the right hand side of each equation by the common denominator.

Among the candidates who obtained honours we had many instances of excellent work and evidence of careful teaching.

Junior Grade.—Girls.

Report of Rev. Francis Lennon, D.D.

With two or three exceptions, there has been very little really good answering in the Junior Girls Algebra. Most of the students have yet to learn how to use their eyes in detecting forms to which well-known principles may be applied. The second question on the paper, for instance, has been answered by a larger number than any other; but in the majority of cases a whole page or more has been devoted to it; whereas by changing the order of factors and applying the familiar formula for the difference of two squares, it might have been answered in four lines.

Junior Grade.—Boys (Over-age).

Report of Rev. Francis Lennon, D.D.

About a dozen over-age boys have answered remarkably well in Junior Grade Algebra; but most of the others ought to present themselves the next time in the Preparatory Grade.

---

6. Find the Lowest Common Multiple of—

$$x^3-x^2-4x+4,\ x^3+2x^2-x-2,\ \text{and}\ x^3-3x-2.$$

7. Find x from the equation—

$$a(cx+2d)(cx+b)^2=c(ax+2b)(ax+d)^2.$$

8. Solve the equation—

$$\frac{2x}{x+2}-\frac{x-17}{4x-8}=\frac{2x}{x-1}+\frac{3x-4}{2x+4}-\frac{7}{4}.$$

9. Find the values of x and y that satisfy the equations—

$$\frac{7}{x+y}+\frac{3}{x-y}=25,$$
$$\frac{3}{x+y}+\frac{5}{x-y}=16.$$

10 Find x and y, in their simplest forms, from the equations—

$$(a+b)^2x-(a+c)^2y=b-c,$$
$$b^2(a+b)x-c^2(a+c)y=b^3-c^3.$$

11. A woman selling apples, sells half her stock and one more to A, one-third of the remainder and two more to B, and one-third of what then remains and three more to C; 25 apples are left. How many had she originally?

12. Two cyclists, A and B, ride a race, the course being from P to Q, a distance of 18 miles and back. A gives B a start of 15 minutes, and meets him on his return journey 1,660 yards from Q, afterwards winning the race by 1 minute. Find the rate at which each cyclist rides, assuming it uniform throughout.

* PREPARATORY GRADE.—BOYS.

Report of Rev. M. BARRETT, THOMAS W. LEWOOD, B.A., and WM. M'F. ORR, M.A.

The answering of the Preparatory Grade Boys was good. The candidates on the whole showed a highly satisfactory knowledge of addition, subtraction, multiplication, and division, while many of them factorised and manipulated rather difficult expressions with wonderful skill.

---

* 1. If $a=9$, $b=5$, $c=3$, and $d=8$, find the value of

$$\frac{c}{\sqrt{a}}+\frac{1}{15}\left(\frac{b}{3}\right)^3-\frac{3}{40}c^2-2\frac{1}{4}\sqrt[3]{\frac{1}{d^2}}-\frac{ad}{b^3}.$$

2. (*a*) Add together—

$$x^3-\frac{5}{8}x^2y-\frac{5}{8}xy^2-\frac{13}{18}y^3$$

$$x^2y+\frac{1}{8}xy^2+\frac{1}{6}y^3-\frac{1}{8}x^3$$

$$xy^2+\frac{5}{12}y^3-\frac{1}{3}x^3+\frac{15}{8}x^2y.$$

(*b*) To what expression must the sum be added to produce

$$\frac{1}{8}x^3+\frac{1}{8}x^2y-\frac{1}{8}xy^2-\frac{1}{8}y^3?$$

3. Multiply—

$$x^3-7x+6 \text{ by } x^2-2x-8.$$

4. Divide—

$$6x^5-x^4-28x^3+5x^2+20x-4 \text{ by } 5x^2+8x-2.$$

5. Divide—

$$x^4-x^2(2a^2+b^2)-b^2(2ax+a^2)+a^4 \text{ by } x+a.$$

6. Reduce to its simplest form—

$$\frac{1+3x}{4(1+x)(1+2x)}-\frac{1+2x}{(1+x)(1+3x)}+\frac{1+x}{4(1+2x)(1+3x)}.$$

7. Simplify—

$$\frac{\frac{x+y}{x-y}+\frac{x-y}{x+y}}{\frac{x-y}{x+y}-\frac{x+y}{x-y}}+\frac{\frac{1}{x^2}+\frac{1}{y^2}}{\frac{y}{x}-\frac{x}{y}}.$$

8. Find the simplest form of—

$$\left(1-\frac{a}{b}+\frac{b}{a}-\frac{b^2}{a^2}\right)\left(\frac{a+b}{2a}+\frac{a-b}{2b}\right)$$

divided by

$$(a+b)\left(a-2b+\frac{b^2}{a}\right)\left(\frac{a}{a+b}+\frac{b}{a-b}\right).$$

9. Find the Highest Common Factor of—

$$6x^3-16x^2-41x-20 \text{ and } x^3-5x^2-25x-28$$

10. Find the Lowest Common Multiple of—

$$x^2-y^2,\ x^4-y^4, \text{ and } x^4+x^2y^2+y^4$$

11. Simplify—

$$\frac{(a-b)^2\{a^2+a(b-c)-bc\}}{(a^2-b^2)\{a^2-a(b+c)+bc\}}.$$

12. Reduce to its simplest form—

$$\frac{\frac{a}{b}+\frac{b}{a}+\frac{x}{y}+\frac{y}{x}}{\frac{a}{b}-\frac{b}{a}+\frac{x}{y}-\frac{y}{x}}.$$

A large number of the candidates omitted the first question altogether, and of those who attempted it comparatively few answered it perfectly. The second, third, fourth, and fifth questions were very well done, though in the fifth some candidates did not understand the brackets, and some did not arrange their work in proper order with regard to powers of x. In the sixth question errors in reducing to a common denominator were frequent. The style of the answers given to the seventh and eighth questions was as a rule very bad, even when the correct results were obtained. The work was generally crowded together without proper arrangement or any explanation of what was being done, and there was an excessive and unnecessary amount of crossing out by way of cancelling. From these causes it was in many cases difficult or even impossible to follow the work. Some of the boys also seemed to think they could change the signs of an expression throughout without altering its value. The ninth question was creditably done on the whole; a few boys factorized the expressions just sufficiently to find a common factor without proving it was the highest. The most common mistakes in the tenth question were due to ignorance of the factors of the last of the three expressions in it. The remarks made about cancelling apply also to the eleventh question, and it was noticeable in this and the twelfth question that many candidates simplified a fraction by subtracting the same quantity from the numerator and denominator.

PREPARATORY GRADE.—GIRLS.

Report of THOMAS W. INWOOD, B.A.

I consider the results of this examination to be decidedly satisfactory. The number of candidates who obtained honours was perhaps smaller than might have been expected, but on the other hand there were not many extremely weak papers, and the work was written out clearly and neatly by most of those examined. Facility in resolving into factors was shown by a considerable number of the students. The answer to the tenth question showed that many had not grasped the meaning of the Lowest Common Multiple. Other mistakes of common occurrence have been referred to in the report on the answering of the boys of the same Grade.

ARITHMETIC.

MIDDLE GRADE.—BOYS OF THE PRESCRIBED AGE.

Report of Ven. C. K. IRWIN, D.D.

The answering in this Grade was decidedly poor. Questions involving thought or knowledge of the theory of a rule were either passed over unattempted, or if attempted were worked in a manner which showed but too plainly that the candidate was groping in the dark.

I have to comment very severely on the carelessness and untidiness of a very large proportion of the work sent up. With a few praiseworthy exceptions neatness does not appear to have been at all attended to in preparation for the examination. In many cases the want of neatness made it extremely difficult to ascertain what purported to be the answer, or indeed whether the candidate considered that he had worked out the question at all.

I may remark that Question 6* was attempted by few, and correctly worked out by only six. On the other hand some papers showed careful teaching and an intelligent grasp of the subjects examined in, and were refreshingly neat and tidily executed.

Having in mind that many of these boys are supposed to contemplate a commercial or business life, I would earnestly impress upon teachers and pupils that much more attention be paid to (*a*.) Spelling, (*b*.) Handwriting, and (*c*.) Neatness of formation of figures.

Middle Grade (Boys Over-age).

Report of S. FitzPatrick.

The answering on the whole was very fair, in many cases it was exceedingly good. The work was neatly executed, and the thinking that is so commonly required in Arithmetic was sound and well-ordered.

Nearly all took the number of shillings in No. 7† to be the square of the side instead of the cube.

Their method of dealing with the reduction of mixed repetends was faulty.

Middle Grade—Girls.

Report of S. FitzPatrick.

The answering in this paper was very moderate. Knowledge of even ordinary rules was wanting, and very few showed any power of dealing with problems. Evidence of somewhat earnest preparation was given by about 25 per cent., the others depended largely on their acquaintance with the subject in the earlier Grades.

Explanation of arithmetical terms was unsatisfactory. In simplifying No. 2, scarcely one saw that $4\cdot\dot{3}57142\dot{8}$ was equal to 4·84. They reduced in the ordinary way, filling pages, and *yet* rarely getting a correct answer. In such questions the answers should not be given in an unfinished decimal form.

In No. 14‡, instead of making a compound proportion statement from first income with rates and prices, they ascertain what stock is purchased, then sell it, and again find what new stock is purchased, from this they find new income. There is no necessity for bringing stock into it. It increases the work and does not prepare the pupil for dealing with really hard questions.

---

* "6. Six per cent. bonds are for sale when the ordinary rate of interest is 5 per cent.; if the bonds are to be redeemed at par at the end of three years, what is their true value? Simple interest to be used in computation."

† "7. A picture whose length was equal to its breadth was sold for £1,066 6s. As many shillings as there were inches in the length of the side of the picture were given for each square inch of the surface, find the length of the side of the picture."

‡ "14. A person invests £18,250 in the 3 per Cents. at 89¼, and sells out when they have risen to 91⅛, and invests the proceeds in 4 per Cents. at 112½. Find the change in his income. Brokerage one-eighth per cent. to be included in each transaction."

Junior Grade.—Boys of the Prescribed Age.

Report of S. FitzPatrick and Rev. Wm. Hughes, D.D.

We have examined the answer books of 2,629 boys, and are enabled to report most favourably. The great majority gives evidence of continued excellent teaching. The boys are thoroughly acquainted with the rules and leading principles of Arithmetic, and most accurate in their calculations; and show a marked improvement in dealing with questions that demand serious thought to determine what process of solution to follow.

The work on the whole is clear and satisfactory; yet there are too many who crowd the pages with figures, and leave the answers hidden and unmarked. Scribbling is very often found on the backs of any page, and even on the blotting paper. An examiner frequently finds it necessary to look to the scribbling to satisfy himself on some point, and expects to find it near the particular sum. A margin of two inches to the right of the page should always be used for this purpose.

The methods of solution were in many cases very roundabout.

In No. 6*, instead of the simple statement of 3200 : 1000, most involved methods were followed, leading eventually to a wrong answer.

In No. 14†, they attempted to extract the cube root of ·29̇6̇ as a decimal, instead of bringing it to the fraction $\frac{8}{27}$; and so with the square root of ·02̇7̇.

Junior Grade.—Boys—Over-age.

Report of Ven. C. K. Irwin, D.D.

The answering in this Grade was decidedly better than that in the Junior Grade—girls—also examined by me. And the work—particularly that of the boys—showed more careful preparation and thought, but there is great room for improvement both in neatness of work and accuracy of detail.

Junior Grade.—Girls.

Report of Ven. C. K. Irwin, D.D.

The work was on the whole fairly done, but it was impossible to fail to observe that questions, the solution of which was more a matter of routine, and consequently the result of cram, were in higher request than those which called for exercise of the mental faculties; for example, Question 12‡ (cube root) was attempted, and generally successfully, by a very large proportion of the candidates. Question 13§—square root—was solved correctly by many up to a certain point of the extraction of the root; but the correctness of the solution was fatally

* "6. A regiment of soldiers, 1,000 strong, consumed 5 tons 11 cwts. 2 qrs. 14·4 lbs. of potatoes in 4 days, but on the fourth day 800 soldiers were absent from dinner. What was the daily consumption when all were present?

† "14. Simplify—

$$\sqrt[3]{\cdot 29\dot{6}} - \sqrt{\cdot 02\dot{7}}."$$

‡ "12. Extract the cube root of 29·993266043."

§ "13. The area of a square field is 1,800 acres 2 roods 20 perches; find the length of a side."

marred by the fact that the candidates, with surprising unanimity, regarded the square root as square *measure*, bringing lineal perches to acres, roods, and perches. Questions involving thought were, as a rule, not satisfactorily worked.

Much more attention should be paid to neatness of handwriting and to formation of figures.

PREPARATORY GRADE.—BOYS.

Report of REV. WM. HUGHES, B.D., and GEORGE B. O'CONNOR, B.A.

The answering on the whole in this section was satisfactory. A few pupils solved every question; those who gained honours formed a high per-centage, while the failures were few—absolutely and relatively. "Cancelling" was not made use of to the extent one would expect. A vagueness as to the meaning of the terms G.C.M. and L.C.M. seems to have prevailed amongst a large number of the pupils. There was a lack of care shown by many in not placing over the question its proper number; in some cases the wrong number appeared—in others there was no number. In many instances the answers were marked so as "to catch" at once the eye of the examiner: in too many cases it was necessary to exert considerable research in order to find them. We may observe that when an effort of reasoning more than usual was required in the solution of a question, such a question was generally avoided. This we attribute to the youth of the pupils rather than to any want of skill or attention on the part of their teachers.

PREPARATORY GRADE.—GIRLS.

Report of EDWARD T. O'BRIEN.

I am much pleased with the answering generally. The candidates showed all through an earnestness and industry which is greatly to their credit, and their knowledge of the subject (particularly for such youthful students) speaks well for their careful training. There were none of the questions on the paper which were not correctly worked out by some of the candidates, many going through the whole paper with great success. The more difficult questions were often attacked and worked out with ease by many who stumbled over the least difficult, which latter fact may be due to not appreciating the meaning of the questions asked, although they only required a little thought. Taking the work all-round it was very good, and there were less than the usual number of actual know-nothings who go in unprepared.

BOOK-KEEPING.

MIDDLE GRADE.—BOYS.

Report of EDWARD T. O'BRIEN.

I regret I cannot speak so favourably of the work in this Grade as of the Junior. The answering was not generally up to a sufficiently high standard. I have little hesitation in saying that the candidates in the Junior Grade showed, upon the whole, quite as much acquaintance with the subject as those in the Middle Grade. There were of course many careful workers, who were well-taught and answered expectations, but the percentage of successful candidates was not sufficient. I should be glad to see more attention given to this grade of book-keeping which covers only, in a very limited way, the usual business of a merchant's office.

MIDDLE GRADE.—GIRLS.

Report of EDWARD T. O'BRIEN.

My remarks with reference to boys in this Grade applies equally to girls. Looking at their success in the lower Grade I naturally expected to find a corresponding degree of success in this Grade but such is not the case. That they have the aptitude for the acquirement of a science so necessary for success in life from a commercial point of view is certain, and if the Junior Grade girls of this year apply themselves to develop further the knowledge they have acquired, their success next year in this Grade would be assured. I must not omit, however, to congratulate those who have succeeded; many of them doing good work.

JUNIOR GRADE.—BOYS.

Report of EDWARD T. O'BRIEN.

I have pleasure in reporting that these students did very fairly well a fair percentage having answered very creditably. There is, however, a good deal of room for improvement, particularly as regards neatness, which is so essential in this subject. Some of the work showed to disadvantage in this respect even where the candidates were otherwise well prepared. At the same time there were very many specimens of good clerkly style which were in every way praiseworthy and spoke well for the teaching. The industry and attention of the candidates generally were good, the actual blanks were few, and there were not many instances of carelessness.

JUNIOR GRADE.—GIRLS.

Report of EDWARD T. O'BRIEN.

The answering of the Junior Grade girls greatly excelled my expectations. I presume from the small number who presented themselves, only those who were well prepared came forward. I regret however that a greater number did not apply themselves to the subject, as those I examined in this Grade showed, with few exceptions, great aptitude for it, and in very many instances a finished style which spoke well for their careful training. The girls' work in this subject and Grade is generally much superior to that of the boys. The number who did not succeed in passing forms a very small percentage, while many have succeeded admirably.

NATURAL PHILOSOPHY.

SENIOR GRADE.—BOYS.

Report of J. JOLY, D.SC., F.R.S.

The answering in the Senior Grade is satisfactory; the questions are, however, easier than those of the previous year, as it was thought that the latter were somewhat above the general level of the students. Judging from the answers received this year, the questions set have fairly tested the preparation of the students. The Examiner in this Grade is of opinion that any attempt at preparation for a higher standard should not be attempted at the early age of the candidates, and should not be necessitated by the nature of the questions. Only the most general laws and simple numerical exercises should constitute the theoretical training. The practical teaching should relate only to the most important experiments. In short very little should be attempted, but what is done should be thoroughly done.

The necessity of practical teaching the Examiner would earnestly impress upon teachers. The neglect of this is very apparent in the answers received to the questions referring to the use of the narrow slit in the spectroscope. There is no more congenial occupation to boys than setting up apparatus, and making experiments. Very cheap and simple apparatus suffice in many cases. In the case alluded to a few simple articles (slit, lens, and prism), would have secured students against depicting the red rays as the most refrangible, or the deviation in the wrong direction.

It is strongly urged that the student should use the apparatus himself. He should be given an experiment to make up, and called upon to repeat and explain it to the teacher. Two or three experiments mastered in the week would mean rapid advance in the study of the subject. Physics cannot be taught according to the traditional methods of teaching—it appeals to quite different mental qualities than do chemical or even mathematical training. The fact that it is simply a training in "common sense" constitutes its great value.

MIDDLE GRADE.—BOYS AND GIRLS.

Report of GEORGE COFFEY, B.E.

The answering in the Middle Grade did not compare favourably with that of the Junior Grade. The preparation does not appear to be so thorough, and attention does not appear to be given to general principles and the common sense of observation. Fully fifty per cent. of the answers to Question No. 1* were to the effect that a kite rises in the air because it is lighter, bulk for bulk, than air! In the case of the better prepared students it was pleasing to note that the mixed units in Questions 9† and 10‡ did not prove a difficulty.

---

* "1. Explain why a kite rises in the air. What is the use of the tail? Illustrate your answer by a diagram of forces."

† "9. A mass of copper weighing 8 lbs. is cooled from 212° F. in an ice calorimeter; the weight of water thereby produced is found to be 0·49 lbs. What is the specific heat of copper? [The latent heat of ice may be taken as 79 thermal units.]

"What are the sources of error generally attending the method of melting ice in calorimeters?"

‡ "10. Two pounds of water are evaporated at 212° F. The latent heat of steam being 537 thermal units, and Joule's equivalent 772 foot lbs. What is the work equivalent of the heat required to evaporate the water?"

JUNIOR GRADE.—BOYS AND GIRLS.

Report of GEORGE COFFEY, B.E., and J. JOLY, D.SC., F.R.S.

The answering in the Junior Grade was on the whole satisfactory, many of the papers showing careful preparation of the subject, and considerable power of thinking out the problems. It is deserving of notice that the question on the principle of the barometer was correctly answered in a majority of instances. In previous years the answers given to questions on the barometer showed in most cases an utter failure to understand the principle of the instrument.

CHEMISTRY.

JUNIOR, MIDDLE, AND SENIOR GRADES.—BOYS AND GIRLS.

Report of RICHARD J. MOSS, F.C.S., F.I.C.

The answering in Chemistry presented the same general features in each of the three Grades. Such questions as simply tested the memory of the student were, as a rule, exactly answered, and the answers were singularly uniform, the words of the text-book being often accurately quoted. Questions involving reasoning, however simple the facts or principles concerned, were not so well answered. Very few students would have failed to state correctly the composition of the atmosphere if the question were asked directly; but when asked to solve a simple problem involving this knowledge they failed in the attempt, with rare exceptions. It is evident that the kind of knowledge they possess is not that practical kind capable of useful application. Except in a few cases, I could detect no evidence of a practical study of the science. This, I think, is greatly to be deplored. The proper study of Chemistry affords mental training of great value. It cultivates in a special degree the habit of accurate observation, and offers peculiar facilities for the practice of inductive reasoning; while, at the same time, the facts learned have a direct bearing upon most of those phenomena of nature with which we come in contact in every-day life. Unless the science is studied experimentally it seems to me to offer no advantages over the study of such a subject as History, in which great proficiency may be attained by mere reading, aided by a retentive memory.

DRAWING.

OBJECT DRAWING.

SENIOR GRADE.

Report of THOMAS M. LINDSAY.

BOYS.

The average character of work in this Grade is far from being good.

In too many cases it is evident that the candidate has hurried the preliminary drawing in order to proceed to the shading, forgetting that a correct outline is indispensable.

In the majority of the drawings, the perspective of the sheet of paper is quite wrong.

Some candidates have added elaborate backgrounds, these must have taken considerable time, they encroach upon the drawing and are altogether valueless.

GIRLS.

The standard of the girls' work is higher than that of the boys.

The remarks with reference to hasty drawing, incorrect perspective, and the introduction of backgrounds, also apply to the girls' work. In several drawings the table on which the group was placed has been included, making the group of objects ridiculously small.

PERSPECTIVE AND PROJECTION OF SHADOWS, ETC.

SENIOR GRADE.—BOYS AND GIRLS.

Report of JOHN CARROLL.

The exercises in this Grade, though not very satisfactory, are somewhat better than those I last reported on, certainly in the perspective portion of the paper, which is again more frequently attempted and with better results than the questions dealing with the projection of shadows. The girls supply a large proportion of good papers, but the boys have a slightly higher proportion of the highest marked papers.

FREEHAND.

MIDDLE GRADE.—BOYS.

Report of THOMAS M. LINDSAY.

The results in this Grade are entirely satisfactory, a remarkable set of papers having been sent in. In these the great majority are freely and correctly drawn with a firm hand, and show a correct estimate of the proportions, an appreciation of the subtleties of curvature, and a nice discrimination of the lesser details.

MIDDLE GRADE.—GIRLS.

Report of EDWARD S. O'BRIEN, B.E.

The drawings examined in this Grade reached a very high average class, quite a number being so remarkable for beauty and clearness of outline that better work, in this respect, could hardly be desired.

Many, too, showed a most commendable degree of accuracy in their work, though in this there is much room for improvement.

Though the example was well calculated to test the candidate's resources to the full, yet, judging from the large numbers of completed drawings sent in, it does not seem to have been found unduly hard.

Altogether the results of this examination are very satisfactory and must be taken as highly creditable both to teachers and pupils.

Practical Geometry.

Middle Grade.—Boys and Girls.

Report of Thomas M. Lindsay.

I have to report that with comparatively few exceptions, there is a want of nicety and exactness in the working out of the problems. In many cases the instruments used have evidently been of an inferior character, and in some, the work has been done entirely by hand.

The section dealing with the "projection of lines and planes," appears to have been insufficiently taught, numbers of papers showing no attempt at solution.

The answering in solid Geometry, however, is generally good, though there is in too many cases a confusion between a pyramid and a prism. Comparatively few candidates seem to understand the meaning of a "vertical" section. In isometric projection a large number have quite ignored the *thickness* of the bottom of the trough (No. 7).*

In few papers have the whole of the questions been attempted, and only one has obtained full marks for No. 6.†

Freehand.

Junior Grade.—Boys of the Prescribed Age.

Report of John Carroll and Thomas M. Lindsay.

We have much pleasure in reporting that a large proportion of the drawings in this Grade are decidedly good, not a few showing marked ability.

There has been less evasion of the rules regarding mechanical assistance than in former years.

There are, however, too many cases showing a want of knowledge of construction, and in several exercises only one side has been attempted.

Proportion, the most essential feature of a good drawing, has, in some few instances, been entirely ignored.

Junior Grade.—Girls of the Prescribed Age.

Report of John Carroll.

The general excellence of the freehand drawing in this Grade is maintained, and there are fewer cases than in former years of unprepared candidates presenting themselves for examination.

The most striking feature in the majority of the papers is the extreme neatness of line with which the drawings are completed. This, however, has been carried out, in too many instances, at the sacrifice of other and more important considerations, i.e., the *proportion* and *balance of form* of the example. To attempt a neat finish or to apply a fine

* "7. Draw the isometric projection of a trough 8′ long, 3′ wide, 1′ deep outside measure, and 3″ thick; scale one-twelfth."

† "6. A cube of 2″ edge stands on a plane, which makes an angle of 30° with H.P., with one edge in H.P. and making an angle of 15° with X.Y. Give plan and elevation."

line to a drawing, which is out of proportion and balance, seems to me much the same as trying to beautify or decorate a house of weak construction, built on a bad foundation.

Though I have no wish to discourage neatness of line and finish of execution, yet it is necessary that students should be led to see that this should not precede the more important considerations which have been pointed out in former reports and which cannot be too often insisted on.

Junior Grade.—Boys and Girls.—Over-age.

Report of Edward S. O'Brien, B.E.

The work of the girls in this Grade is, all through, somewhat better than that of the boys, though both maintain a good average in their marks.

The percentage of boys sending in very poor work is larger than it should be, being about three times that of the girls.

. Though a large number of candidates obtained very good marks, yet, no drawings of exceptional merit were sent in.

The example set was very suitable and evidently by no means difficult for a well prepared student to finish in the allotted time.

Many candidates seem to fill in details before they finish the general lines of the subject, usually with the result of a much distorted drawing.

Altogether much good work was done and considerable evidence of good teaching was evinced throughout the examination.

Practical Geometry.

Junior Grade.—Boys.

Report of John Carroll and Edward S. O'Brien, B.E.

We consider the result of the examination very satisfactory. The majority of the candidates were evidently better prepared than in former years, although fewer have succeeded in reaching the maximum number of marks given for this subject.

The solutions of problems Nos. 3* and 6†, given to test the student's power of drawing neatly and accurately, were generally good, but we regret to state that the solutions to Question No. 5‡, dealing with areas, were rarely correct, many candidates satisfying themselves with merely finding a *parallelogram* of equal area to the triangle.

The question on the construction of *scales* was seldom accurately finished, though that dealing with the *application* of scales was in the majority of cases quite correct. Many marks were lost through the misplacing of zero on the scale, and not a few others were deducted through the omission of the names of the divisions and subdivisions, *i.e.*, *feet* and *inches*.

Questions dealing with the projection of solids were, when attempted, well answered as far as the solids were concerned, but their *sections* were not often represented correctly.

---

* "3. On a line 1 inch long construct an equilateral triangle. Describe three equal circles, each having its centre in a corner of the triangle, and having a radius of half an inch."

† "6. Within a regular octagon whose diagonal is 9 inches long inscribe the largest possible square."

‡ "5. Construct a square equal in area to the triangle in question 3."

JUNIOR GRADE.—GIRLS.

Report of ALICE M. KEOGH.

Some of the papers could not be excelled in neatness; but this cannot be said of the majority, for the students' work shows that they do not appreciate the necessity of neatness and exactness in Geometry.

The answering of the scale question, which was very simple, was not as good as might have been expected, for the reason that many failed to see its simplicity.

It may be as well to mention here that answers should only be worked on one side of the paper, and that without the use of instruments it is not possible to work out problems properly.

FREEHAND.

PREPARATORY GRADE.—BOYS.

Report of ALICE M. KEOGH.

The average in this Grade was fair, and a great many more succeeded in representing the character of the object than last year; but in many cases, and where evidently it was not due to lack of ability on the student's part, the work was weak, the character and proportion being sacrificed to the erroneous idea that *outline* is of the first importance.

No doubt without a neat, firm outline a freehand drawing is deficient in beauty and completeness, yet outline—to repeat the remark I made last year—done over a poor form has little value. Therefore if students would devote a little more of the allotted time in examination to the consideration of the general shape and the proportion of the example and when they have got these satisfactorily, *then* proceed to finish with a neat line, the result would be that they could not fail to obtain higher marks.

Again, this time a number of drawings were sent in done by candidates who cannot have studied in this subject at all, the drawings being very rude and clumsy, sometimes careless.

A small percentage lost marks by ignoring the instructions not to use mechanical means, and to enlarge the copy; some even reducing it.

PREPARATORY GRADE.—GIRLS.

Report of EDWARD S. O'BRIEN, B.B.

A very large amount of good steady work was done in this Grade, together with a fair number of drawings of great excellence.

Nearly all the candidates seemed to have honestly worked during the time of examination, a fact which must be considered very creditable to both students and teachers, especially when the youth of the former is taken into consideration.

The example was evidently a fair test, and easy to finish within the time allowed.

Some students neglected, or had not been taught, to make use of a "centre line" when working, consequently their drawings often showed a lack of symmetry which much reduced their marks. Others would do well to become familiar with the amount of enlargement required, and not attempt a size much too large for their paper.

No amount of careful finish will cover faulty and unsymmetrical outline—a point which all should remember, but especially those who work slowly.

This is a matter in which teachers might be able to effect an improvement by requiring more time to be spent, than is at present, by the pupils in obtaining a correct outline when employed at "term-tests," &c.

SHORTHAND.

Junior, Middle, and Senior Grades.—Boys and Girls.

Report of M. F. Boyle and George Wm. Bunbury.

We have to report with reference to the Shorthand examination as follows:—Two papers were set, A. Paper, Longhand into Shorthand; and B. Paper, a passage in Shorthand to be transcribed. 150 marks were assigned to each paper. The answering was characterised by great unevenness; not a few of the papers reached a high standard of excellence, while a considerable number, especially in the Junior Grade, failed to secure a Pass; on the whole the work can only be considered as fairly satisfactory.

A. Paper (Longhand into Shorthand).—The principle of phonetics was in many instances scarcely sufficiently understood, certain of the candidates reproducing by phonographic symbols the longhand letters instead of the sounds of the words. We observed a curious frequency of the intersected and circle vowel signs, as well as of the w and y series of diphthongs, as if the pupils were aware of the importance of the principles, but were not familiar with their application. Attention must be called to the fact that some of the papers exhibited ignorance of recent alterations in the system, such archaisms being found as the half-length "s" for such words as "sight," "set," &c., and the consonant stroke "h" for "he," &c. Teachers should see to this, and keep their own knowledge of the system, as well as their candidates, thoroughly up to date.

B. Paper (Shorthand to be transcribed).—A want of sufficient reading practice was clearly indicated. For beginners, as distinct from expert writers, practice in reading shorthand is almost as useful as in writing it. We strongly recommend pupils to devote a certain amount of time to reading printed, lithographed, or even well-written manuscript shorthand in the style suited to their Grade. It will familiarise them with the grammalogues and contractions, the proper outlines, phrasing, &c. In reading (or transcribing) shorthand notes the sense of the passage should always be kept in mind; the context often determines the correct transcription of an outline. Many errors occurred which might have been avoided if this matter had been attended to.

We desire particularly to call the attention of teachers and pupils to the following. While every reasonable effort should be made so as to secure as neat and careful work as possible, too much time should not be expended in this direction. We noticed many of the candidates this year commenced their work at much too slow a rate to enable them to get through even a fair percentage of it in the time, and, consequently, we deem it advisable to call attention to this matter.

MUSIC.

Junior, Middle, and Senior Grades.—Girls only.

Report of Thomas Gick, mus.d.

Junior Grade.

Notation, intervals, musical signs, and the major scales were well answered. The minor scales were not so well answered; many of the students appeared to be unacquainted with that form of the minor containing the step of an augmented second and termed the "chromatic mode."

Time and accent.—In a few instances only students obtained full marks.

Harmony.—With few exceptions the answering was not good. Students in filling in the harmonies of the exercise in figured bass, did not appear to be acquainted with the resolution of the Dominant 7th and its inversions, or when they made objectionable "false relations."

As a *general rule*, in order to get a smooth progression of parts, it is advisable that a note forming part of a chord, and which has appeared in the preceding chord, should be retained in the same part. Instead of this, care seemed to be taken to avoid any such connecting link, with the result that extremely ugly—and vocally impossible—skips were made.

The general answering, with the exception of the questions in harmony, was good. While giving this merited praise, I cannot avoid coming to the conclusion that the attention of the students appears to be chiefly directed to those branches in the theory of music most easily acquired to the neglect of the study of the construction and progression of chords, a knowledge of which would serve them so much as singers or instrumentalists.

Middle Grade.

Notation, intervals, time and accent were fairly well answered. In the minor scales some of the students in this as well as the Junior Grade, fell into the error of giving chromatic *scales*, instead of minor scales in the chromatic *mode*.

History of music.—Most of the answers in this part of the subject were weak; especially so in the names given as the writers of well-known works.

Transposition.—The answering was very good.

Harmony.—The exercise in figured bass was not, generally, so well answered; the progression of parts in some instances were awkward, from the same cause as that mentioned in the Junior Grade.

Taking a general view of the answering in this Grade, it reflects credit upon the students, who showed an intelligent and general knowledge of the subject.

Senior Grade.—Girls only.

Report of Thomas Gick, mus.d.

Notation, time and accent, and *musical terms.*—The answering was fairly good.

History of music.—The answering, with few exceptions, was very bad.

Form.—This question dealt merely with the "outline" of the fugue form of composition. Very few of the students appeared to have any conception of this important form, and the answering was consequently not satisfactory.

Transposition was generally well answered.

Harmony and *counterpoint* exercises were fairly well done.

With reference to these exercises, students are in the habit of first writing their answers in "short score," subsequently rewriting in "open score," with the C clef for all the parts above the bass; and not being sufficiently experienced in its use—particularly for the soprano—they fall into errors, thereby losing both marks and valuable time.

I would strongly advise the disuse of the C clef for the soprano, and that students should accustom themselves, *during their studies*, to the use of the "open score" for their counterpoint exercise.

BOTANY.

Junior, Middle, and Senior Grades.—Girls only.

Report of Henry H. Dixon, B.A.

The answering in Botany, on the whole, indicates much painstaking work both on the part of students and teachers, and the percentage of passes is good. From the style of the papers, however, it is but too evident that the candidates' knowledge of the work is derived almost altogether from text-books, and is seldom supplemented to any extent by observation. The excessive use of technical terms without an exact comprehension of their meaning is very frequent, and appears in many cases only to obscure the candidates' ignorance from themselves, and prevents them using their powers of observation and description. These faults are much more apparent in the Senior than in the Middle and Junior Grades.

LIST OF SCHOOLS TO THE MANAGERS OF WHICH RESULTS FEES WERE PAID IN 18[illegible], AND AMOUNTS OF SUCH FEES.

BOYS.

[illegible]

[illegible]	[illegible]	[illegible]	[illegible]	[illegible]	[illegible]
			£ s. d.	£ s. d.	£ s. d.
[illegible]	[illegible]	[illegible]	[illegible]	[illegible]	[illegible]
	[illegible]	[illegible]	[illegible]	[illegible]	[illegible]
	Do.	[illegible]	[illegible]	[illegible]	[illegible]
	Do.	The Academy,	—	[illegible]	[illegible]
	[illegible]	[illegible]	[illegible]	[illegible]	[illegible]
	[illegible]	[illegible]	[illegible]	[illegible]	[illegible]
[illegible]	[illegible]	[illegible]	[illegible]	[illegible]	[illegible]
	Do.	[illegible]	[illegible]	[illegible]	[illegible]
	Do.	[illegible]	[illegible]	[illegible]	[illegible]
	Do.	[illegible]	[illegible]	[illegible]	[illegible]
	Do.	Do. [illegible]	[illegible]	[illegible]	[illegible]
	Do.	Do. [illegible]	[illegible]	[illegible]	[illegible]
	Do.	Do. [illegible]	[illegible]	[illegible]	[illegible]

[illegible]

[illegible]

BOYS.

[illegible]	[illegible]	[illegible]	[illegible]	[illegible]	[illegible]
		[illegible]	[illegible]	[illegible]	[illegible]
[illegible]	[illegible]	[illegible]	[illegible]	[illegible]	[illegible]
	Do.	[illegible]	[illegible]	[illegible]	[illegible]
	[illegible]	[illegible]	[illegible]	[illegible]	[illegible]
	Do.	[illegible]	[illegible]	[illegible]	[illegible]
	Do.	[illegible]	[illegible]	[illegible]	[illegible]
[illegible]	[illegible]	[illegible]	[illegible]	[illegible]	[illegible]
	[illegible]	[illegible]	[illegible]	[illegible]	[illegible]
[illegible]	[illegible]	[illegible]	[illegible]	[illegible]	[illegible]
	[illegible]	[illegible]	[illegible]	[illegible]	[illegible]
[illegible]	[illegible]	[illegible]	[illegible]	[illegible]	[illegible]
	[illegible]	[illegible]	[illegible]	[illegible]	[illegible]
	[illegible]	[illegible]	[illegible]	[illegible]	[illegible]
[illegible]	[illegible]	[illegible]	[illegible]	[illegible]	[illegible]
	[illegible]	do.	[illegible]	[illegible]	[illegible]
	[illegible]	do.	[illegible]	[illegible]	[illegible]
	Do.	[illegible]	[illegible]	[illegible]	[illegible]
	[illegible]	[illegible]	[illegible]	[illegible]	[illegible]
	[illegible]	do.	[illegible]	[illegible]	[illegible]

[illegible]

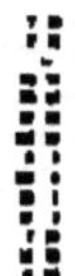

BOYS

[illegible]	Name of School.	[illegible]		
		£	s.	d.
	Brought forward	[illegible]	[illegible]	[illegible]
[illegible]	[illegible]	[illegible]	[illegible]	[illegible]
[illegible]	[illegible]	[illegible]	[illegible]	[illegible]
[illegible]	[illegible]	[illegible]	[illegible]	[illegible]
[illegible]	[illegible]	[illegible]	[illegible]	[illegible]
[illegible]	[illegible]	[illegible]	[illegible]	[illegible]
[illegible]	[illegible]	[illegible]	[illegible]	[illegible]
[illegible]	[illegible]	[illegible]	[illegible]	[illegible]
[illegible]	[illegible]	[illegible]	[illegible]	[illegible]
[illegible]	[illegible]	[illegible]	[illegible]	[illegible]
[illegible]	[illegible]	[illegible]	[illegible]	[illegible]
[illegible]	[illegible]	[illegible]	[illegible]	[illegible]
[illegible]	[illegible]	—		
[illegible]	[illegible]	[illegible]	[illegible]	[illegible]
[illegible]	[illegible]	[illegible]	[illegible]	[illegible]
[illegible]	[illegible]	[illegible]	[illegible]	[illegible]
[illegible]	[illegible]	[illegible]	[illegible]	[illegible]

[illegible]

BOYS.

[illegible]	[illegible]	[illegible]	[illegible]			[illegible]			[illegible]		
			£	s.	d.	£	s.	d.	£	s.	d.
		[illegible]	[illegible]	[illegible]	[illegible]	[illegible]	[illegible]	[illegible]	[illegible]	[illegible]	[illegible]
[illegible]	[illegible]	[illegible]	[illegible]	[illegible]	[illegible]	[illegible]	[illegible]	[illegible]	[illegible]	[illegible]	[illegible]
	Do.	[illegible]	–			[illegible]	[illegible]	[illegible]	[illegible]	[illegible]	[illegible]
	[illegible]	[illegible]	[illegible]	[illegible]	[illegible]	[illegible]	[illegible]	[illegible]	[illegible]	[illegible]	[illegible]
	Do.	[illegible]	[illegible]	[illegible]	[illegible]	[illegible]	[illegible]	[illegible]	[illegible]	[illegible]	[illegible]
	Do.	[illegible]	[illegible]	[illegible]	[illegible]	[illegible]	[illegible]	[illegible]	[illegible]	[illegible]	[illegible]
	Do.	[illegible]	[illegible]	[illegible]	[illegible]	[illegible]	[illegible]	[illegible]	[illegible]	[illegible]	[illegible]
	[illegible]	[illegible]	[illegible]	[illegible]	[illegible]	[illegible]	[illegible]	[illegible]	[illegible]	[illegible]	[illegible]
	[illegible]	[illegible]	[illegible]	[illegible]	[illegible]	[illegible]	[illegible]	[illegible]	[illegible]	[illegible]	[illegible]
[illegible]	[illegible]	[illegible]	[illegible]	[illegible]	[illegible]	[illegible]	[illegible]	[illegible]	[illegible]	[illegible]	[illegible]
	Do.	[illegible]	[illegible]	[illegible]	[illegible]	[illegible]	[illegible]	[illegible]	[illegible]	[illegible]	[illegible]
	Do.	[illegible]	[illegible]	[illegible]	[illegible]	[illegible]	[illegible]	[illegible]	[illegible]	[illegible]	[illegible]
[illegible]	[illegible]	[illegible]	[illegible]	[illegible]	[illegible]	[illegible]	[illegible]	[illegible]	[illegible]	[illegible]	[illegible]

BOYS.
[illegible]

County.	Town.	Name of School.	[illegible]	[illegible]	Total amount paid.
			[illegible]	[illegible]	[illegible]
Clare,	[illegible]	[illegible]	[illegible]	[illegible]	[illegible]
	Do.	[illegible]	[illegible]	[illegible]	[illegible]
	[illegible]	[illegible]	[illegible]	[illegible]	[illegible]
	[illegible]	[illegible]	[illegible]	[illegible]	[illegible]
	[illegible]	[illegible]	[illegible]	[illegible]	[illegible]
Cork,	[illegible]	[illegible]	[illegible]	[illegible]	[illegible]
	[illegible]	[illegible]	[illegible]	[illegible]	[illegible]
	Cork,	Do.	[illegible]	[illegible]	[illegible]
	Do.	[illegible]	[illegible]	[illegible]	[illegible]
	Do.	[illegible]	[illegible]	[illegible]	[illegible]
	Do.	[illegible]	[illegible]	[illegible]	[illegible]
	Do.	[illegible]	[illegible]	[illegible]	[illegible]
	Do.	[illegible]	[illegible]	[illegible]	[illegible]
	[illegible]	[illegible]	[illegible]	[illegible]	[illegible]
	[illegible]	Do.	[illegible]	[illegible]	[illegible]

BOYS.

[illegible]	[illegible]	[illegible]	[illegible]	[illegible]	[illegible]
			£ s. d.	£ s. d.	£ s. d.
		[illegible],	[illegible]	[illegible]	[illegible]
[illegible],	[illegible]	St. [illegible] College,	[illegible]	[illegible]	[illegible]
	[illegible],	[illegible],	[illegible]	[illegible]	[illegible]
	[illegible],	[illegible],	[illegible]	[illegible]	[illegible]
	Do.,	The College,	[illegible]	[illegible]	[illegible]
	Do.,	[illegible] School,	—	[illegible]	[illegible]
	[illegible],	[illegible],	[illegible]	[illegible]	[illegible]
	[illegible],	[illegible] College,	[illegible]	[illegible]	[illegible]
	[illegible],	St. [illegible] College,	[illegible]	[illegible]	[illegible]
	[illegible],	[illegible],	[illegible]	[illegible]	[illegible]
	[illegible],	[illegible],	[illegible]	[illegible]	[illegible]
	[illegible],	[illegible],	[illegible]	[illegible]	[illegible]

BOYS.

BOYS.

[illegible]

[illegible]	[illegible]	[illegible]	[illegible]	[illegible]	[illegible]
[illegible]	[illegible]	[illegible]	[illegible]	[illegible]	[illegible]
	[illegible]	[illegible]	[illegible]	[illegible]	[illegible]
	Do.	[illegible]	[illegible]	[illegible]	[illegible]
	Do.	[illegible]	[illegible]	[illegible]	[illegible]
	[illegible]	[illegible]	[illegible]	[illegible]	[illegible]
	[illegible]	[illegible]	[illegible]	[illegible]	[illegible]
	Do.	[illegible]	[illegible]	[illegible]	[illegible]
[illegible]	[illegible]	[illegible]	[illegible]	[illegible]	[illegible]
[illegible]	[illegible]	[illegible]	[illegible]	[illegible]	[illegible]
	[illegible]	[illegible]	[illegible]	[illegible]	[illegible]
[illegible]	[illegible]	[illegible]	[illegible]	[illegible]	[illegible]
	Do.	[illegible]	[illegible]	[illegible]	[illegible]
	[illegible]	[illegible]	[illegible]	[illegible]	[illegible]

GIRLS.

[illegible]

[illegible]	[illegible]	[illegible]	[illegible]	[illegible]
		£ s. d.	£ s. d.	£ s. d.
[illegible]	[illegible]	[illegible]	[illegible]	[illegible]
[illegible]	[illegible]	[illegible]	[illegible]	[illegible]
[illegible]	[illegible]	[illegible]	[illegible]	[illegible]
[illegible]	[illegible]	[illegible]	[illegible]	[illegible]
[illegible]	[illegible]	[illegible]	[illegible]	[illegible]
[illegible]	[illegible]	—	[illegible]	[illegible]
[illegible]	[illegible]	[illegible]	[illegible]	[illegible]
[illegible]	[illegible]	[illegible]	[illegible]	[illegible]
[illegible]	[illegible]	[illegible]	[illegible]	[illegible]

Name of School.	[illegible]			[illegible]			[illegible]		
	£	s.	d.	£	s.	d.	£	s.	d.
[illegible]	[illegible]	[illegible]	[illegible]	[illegible]	[illegible]	[illegible]	[illegible]	[illegible]	[illegible]
[illegible]	[illegible]	[illegible]	[illegible]	[illegible]	[illegible]	[illegible]	[illegible]	[illegible]	[illegible]
[illegible]	[illegible]	[illegible]	[illegible]	[illegible]	[illegible]	[illegible]	[illegible]	[illegible]	[illegible]
[illegible]	[illegible]	[illegible]	[illegible]	[illegible]	[illegible]	[illegible]	[illegible]	[illegible]	[illegible]
[illegible]	[illegible]	[illegible]	[illegible]	[illegible]	[illegible]	[illegible]	[illegible]	[illegible]	[illegible]
[illegible]	[illegible]	[illegible]	[illegible]	[illegible]	[illegible]	[illegible]	[illegible]	[illegible]	[illegible]
[illegible]	[illegible]	[illegible]	[illegible]	[illegible]	[illegible]	[illegible]	[illegible]	[illegible]	[illegible]
[illegible]	[illegible]	[illegible]	[illegible]	[illegible]	[illegible]	[illegible]	[illegible]	[illegible]	[illegible]
[illegible]	[illegible]	[illegible]	[illegible]	[illegible]	[illegible]	[illegible]	[illegible]	[illegible]	[illegible]
[illegible]	[illegible]	[illegible]	[illegible]	[illegible]	[illegible]	[illegible]	[illegible]	[illegible]	[illegible]
[illegible]	–			[illegible]	[illegible]	[illegible]	[illegible]	[illegible]	[illegible]
[illegible]	[illegible]	[illegible]	[illegible]	[illegible]	[illegible]	[illegible]	[illegible]	[illegible]	[illegible]
[illegible]	[illegible]	[illegible]	[illegible]	[illegible]	[illegible]	[illegible]	[illegible]	[illegible]	[illegible]
[illegible]	[illegible]	[illegible]	[illegible]	[illegible]	[illegible]	[illegible]	[illegible]	[illegible]	[illegible]
[illegible]	[illegible]	[illegible]	[illegible]	[illegible]	[illegible]	[illegible]	[illegible]	[illegible]	[illegible]
[illegible]	[illegible]	[illegible]	[illegible]	[illegible]	[illegible]	[illegible]	[illegible]	[illegible]	[illegible]
[illegible]	[illegible]	[illegible]	[illegible]	[illegible]	[illegible]	[illegible]	[illegible]	[illegible]	[illegible]

[illegible]

GIRLS.

[illegible]	[illegible]	[illegible]	[illegible]	[illegible]	[illegible]
			£ s. d.	£ s. d.	£ s. d.
		[illegible]	[illegible]	[illegible]	[illegible]
[illegible]	[illegible]	[illegible]	[illegible]	[illegible]	[illegible]
	[illegible]	[illegible]	—	[illegible]	[illegible]
	Do.	[illegible]	[illegible]	[illegible]	[illegible]
	Do.	[illegible]	[illegible]	[illegible]	[illegible]
	[illegible]	[illegible]	[illegible]	[illegible]	[illegible]
	[illegible]	[illegible]	[illegible]	[illegible]	[illegible]
	[illegible]	[illegible]	[illegible]	[illegible]	[illegible]
	[illegible]	[illegible]	—	[illegible]	[illegible]
	[illegible]	[illegible]	[illegible]	[illegible]	[illegible]
[illegible]	[illegible]	[illegible]	[illegible]	[illegible]	[illegible]
	Do.	[illegible]	—	[illegible]	[illegible]
[illegible]	[illegible]	[illegible]	[illegible]	[illegible]	[illegible]
[illegible]	[illegible]	[illegible]	[illegible]	[illegible]	[illegible]
[illegible]	[illegible]	[illegible]	[illegible]	[illegible]	[illegible]
[illegible]	[illegible]	[illegible]	[illegible]	[illegible]	[illegible]

[illegible]

GIRLS.

[illegible]	[illegible]	[illegible]	[illegible]	[illegible]	[illegible]
		[illegible]	[illegible]	[illegible]	[illegible]
[illegible]	[illegible]	[illegible]	[illegible]	[illegible]	[illegible]
[illegible]	[illegible]	[illegible]	[illegible]	[illegible]	[illegible]
[illegible]	[illegible]	[illegible]	[illegible]	[illegible]	[illegible]
	[illegible]	[illegible]	[illegible]	[illegible]	[illegible]
	[illegible]	[illegible]	[illegible]	[illegible]	[illegible]
[illegible]	[illegible]	[illegible]	[illegible]	[illegible]	[illegible]
	Do.	[illegible]	[illegible]	[illegible]	[illegible]
	[illegible]	[illegible]		[illegible]	[illegible]
		[illegible]	[illegible]	[illegible]	[illegible]

[illegible]

GIRLS.

[illegible]	[illegible]	[illegible]	[illegible]	[illegible]	[illegible]
[illegible]	[illegible]	[illegible]	[illegible]	[illegible]	[illegible]
	[illegible]	[illegible]	[illegible]	[illegible]	[illegible]
	Do.	[illegible]	[illegible]	[illegible]	[illegible]
	Do.	[illegible]	[illegible]	[illegible]	[illegible]
		[illegible]	[illegible]	[illegible]	[illegible]

[illegible]

GIRLS

[illegible]

[illegible]

GIRLS.

County.	Town.	Name of School.	[illegible]	[illegible]	[illegible]
			£ s. d.	£ s. d.	£ s. d.
		Brought forward,	[illegible]	[illegible]	[illegible]
[illegible]	[illegible]	[illegible]	[illegible]	[illegible]	[illegible]
	Do.	[illegible]	[illegible]	[illegible]	[illegible]
	Do.	[illegible]	[illegible]	[illegible]	[illegible]
	[illegible]	[illegible]	[illegible]	[illegible]	[illegible]
	[illegible]	[illegible]	[illegible]	[illegible]	[illegible]
	Do.	[illegible]	[illegible]	[illegible]	[illegible]
[illegible]	[illegible]	[illegible]	[illegible]	[illegible]	[illegible]
	Do.	[illegible]	[illegible]	[illegible]	[illegible]
	[illegible]	[illegible]	—	[illegible]	[illegible]
	[illegible]	[illegible]	[illegible]	[illegible]	[illegible]
	[illegible]	[illegible]	[illegible]	[illegible]	[illegible]
	[illegible]	[illegible]	[illegible]	[illegible]	[illegible]
[illegible]	[illegible]	[illegible]	[illegible]	[illegible]	[illegible]
	Do.	[illegible]	[illegible]	[illegible]	[illegible]
	[illegible]	[illegible]	[illegible]	[illegible]	[illegible]
	[illegible]	[illegible]	[illegible]	[illegible]	[illegible]
	[illegible]	[illegible]	[illegible]	[illegible]	[illegible]
	[illegible]	[illegible]	[illegible]	[illegible]	[illegible]
	[illegible]	[illegible]	[illegible]	[illegible]	[illegible]
		Carried forward,	[illegible]	[illegible]	[illegible]

List of [illegible] in the [illegible] of which Results Fees were Paid in 18[illegible], and Amount of such Fees—continued.

GIRLS.

County.	Town.	Name of School.	Amount paid [illegible] Head-masters.	Amount paid [illegible] Teachers.	Total amount paid.
			£ s. d.	£ s. d.	£ s. d.
		[illegible]	[illegible]	[illegible]	[illegible]
[illegible]—continued.	[illegible]	Ladies' [illegible] School,	[illegible]	[illegible]	[illegible]
	[illegible]	[illegible] School,	[illegible]	[illegible]	[illegible]
	Do.,	Ladies' School,	[illegible]	[illegible]	[illegible]
	[illegible]	[illegible] School,	[illegible]	[illegible]	[illegible]
Londonderry,	Londonderry,	Ladies' [illegible] School,	[illegible]	[illegible]	[illegible]
	Do.,	Ladies' School, [illegible]	[illegible]	[illegible]	[illegible]
	Do.,	[illegible] School,	[illegible]	[illegible]	[illegible]
	Do.,	[illegible] School,	[illegible]	[illegible]	[illegible]
	[illegible]	[illegible]	[illegible]	[illegible]	[illegible]
	[illegible]	[illegible] School,	[illegible]	[illegible]	[illegible]
[illegible]	[illegible]	Convent of St. Louis,	[illegible]	[illegible]	[illegible]
	Do.,	Ladies' School,	[illegible]	[illegible]	[illegible]
Tyrone,	[illegible]	Ladies' School,	[illegible]	[illegible]	[illegible]
	[illegible]	Ladies' School,	[illegible]	[illegible]	[illegible]
	Do.,	[illegible]	[illegible]	[illegible]	[illegible]
	[illegible]	[illegible] School,	[illegible]	[illegible]	[illegible]
	[illegible]	[illegible] School,	[illegible]	[illegible]	[illegible]
	Do.,	[illegible] Convent,	[illegible]	[illegible]	[illegible]
	[illegible]	[illegible] School,	—	[illegible]	[illegible]
	Do.,	[illegible]	—	[illegible]	[illegible]

GIRLS.

MUNSTER.

County.	Town.	[illegible]	[illegible]	[illegible]	[illegible]
			£ s. d.	£ s. d.	£ s. d.
CLARE,	[illegible]	[illegible]	[illegible]	[illegible]	[illegible]
CORK,	Cork,	[illegible]	[illegible]	[illegible]	[illegible]
	Do.,	[illegible]	[illegible]	[illegible]	[illegible]
	Do.,	[illegible]	[illegible]	[illegible]	[illegible]
	Do.,	[illegible]	[illegible]	[illegible]	[illegible]
	Do.,	[illegible]	[illegible]	[illegible]	[illegible]
	[illegible]	[illegible]	[illegible]	[illegible]	[illegible]
	[illegible]	[illegible]	[illegible]	[illegible]	[illegible]
	[illegible]	[illegible]	[illegible]	[illegible]	[illegible]
	[illegible]	[illegible]	[illegible]	[illegible]	[illegible]
	[illegible]	[illegible]	[illegible]	[illegible]	[illegible]
	Do.,	[illegible]	[illegible]	[illegible]	[illegible]
KERRY,	[illegible]	[illegible]	[illegible]	[illegible]	[illegible]
	[illegible]	[illegible]	[illegible]	[illegible]	[illegible]
LIMERICK,	[illegible]	[illegible]	[illegible]	[illegible]	[illegible]
	[illegible]	[illegible]	[illegible]	[illegible]	[illegible]
	Do.,	[illegible]	[illegible]	[illegible]	[illegible]
	Do.,	[illegible]	[illegible]	[illegible]	[illegible]
TIPPERARY,	[illegible]	[illegible]	[illegible]	[illegible]	[illegible]
WATERFORD,	[illegible]	[illegible]	[illegible]	[illegible]	[illegible]
	Do.,	[illegible]	[illegible]	[illegible]	[illegible]
		Total,	[illegible]	[illegible]	[illegible]

[illegible] [1]

GIRLS.

[illegible]

County.	Town.	Name of School.	[illegible]	[illegible]	[illegible]
			[illegible]	[illegible]	[illegible]
[illegible]	[illegible]	High School,	[illegible]	[illegible]	[illegible]
[illegible]	[illegible]	[illegible]	[illegible]	[illegible]	[illegible]
[illegible]	[illegible]	Intermediate School,	[illegible]	[illegible]	[illegible]
	Do.	[illegible]	[illegible]	[illegible]	[illegible]
	Do.	Loreto Convent,	[illegible]	[illegible]	[illegible]
		Total,	[illegible]	[illegible]	[illegible]

Report of the Intermediate [illegible]

APPENDIX V.

Localities in which Examinations were held.

BOYS.

Localities.	No. of Centres.	Localities.	No. of Centres.
Armagh,	1	Killarney,	3
Athenry,	1	Kilrush,	1
Athlone,	2	Kingstown,	2
Athy,	1	Letterkenny,	1
Ballymena,	1	Limerick,	6
Bangor,	1	Lisburn,	1
Belfast,	10	Lismore,	1
Blackrock,	3	Listowel,	1
Bruff,	1	Londonderry,	4
Cahersiveen,	1	Longford,	1
Callan,	1	Lurgan,	1
Carlow,	3	Mallow,	1
Carrick-on-Suir,	1	Midleton,	2
Cashel,	4	Mitchelstown,	1
Castleknock,	2	Monaghan,	2
Cavan,	1	Mountrath,	1
Charleville,	1	Mullingar,	1
Clongowes Wood College,	3	Multyfarnham,	1
Clonmel,	2	Navan,	1
Clonskeagh,	1	Nenagh,	2
Coleraine,	1	New Ross,	1
Cookstown,	1	Newry,	5
Cork,	19	Omagh,	1
Dingle,	1	Parsonstown,	1
Doneraile,	1	Portarlington,	1
Drogheda,	1	Queenstown,	1
Dublin,	31	Raphoe,	1
Dundalk,	6	Skibbereen,	1
Dungannon,	2	Sligo,	3
Dungarvan,	1	Strabane,	1
Ennis,	2	Terenure,	1
Enniscorthy,	1	Thurles,	1
Enniskillen,	3	Tipperary,	2
Fermoy,	5	Tralee,	2
Galway,	1	Tuam,	3
Gorey,	1	Waterford,	4
Holywood (Down),	1	Westport,	1
Kells,	1	Wexford,	6
Kilkenny,	6	Youghal,	1
		Total,	172

Localities in which Examinations were held—*continued.*

GIRLS.

Localities.	No. of Centres.	Localities.	No. of Centres.
Armagh, ...	1	Letterkenny, . . .	1
Athy, ...	1	Limerick, ...	1
Balbriggan, ...	1	Lisburn, ...	1
Ballymena, ...	1	Londonderry, . . .	3
Ballymoney, ...	1	Longford, ...	1
Belfast, ...	10	Monaghan, ...	1
Blackrock, ...	2	Mountmellick, . . .	1
Bray, ...	1	Mullingar, ...	1
Bruff, ...	1	Navan, ...	1
Coleraine, ...	1	Newry, ...	1
Cookstown, ...	1	Omagh, ...	1
Cork, ...	4	Portadown, . .	1
Dalkey, ...	1	Rathfarnham, . . .	1
Dublin, ...	18	Skibbereen, .	1
Dungannon, . . .	1	Sligo, . . .	2
Enniscorthy, . . .	1	Tralee, . . .	1
Gorey, ...	1	Waterford, .	2
Holywood (Down), . .	1	Wexford, . . .	1
Kilkenny, ...	1		
Killarney, ...	1	Total, . . .	69

Appendix VI.

The Burke Memorial Prizes.

A sum of money, subscribed in memory of the late Thomas Henry Burke, Esq., Under Secretary to the Lord Lieutenant, was transferred by the Burke Memorial Committee, on 18th March, 1881, to the Intermediate Education Board for Ireland, who undertook to administer the Fund in accordance with the following Rules—(the sum funded is £1,332 18s. 11d. Consols):—

I. The annual income from the fund shall be applied in paying three Prizes, one of £16, one of £10, and a second of £10; any surplus or deficiency to be apportioned in the same ratio. If, in the opinion of the Commissioners, sufficient merit be not shown by the Candidates competing to justify the award of any or either of the Prizes, the amount of such Prize may be, at the discretion of the Board, withheld and added to the principal.

II. No student shall be qualified to receive these Prizes except the children of persons who are or have been, in receipt of salary or pension in Ireland, paid out of money derived from Parliamentary Grants, Rates or Taxes, other than members of the Naval or Military Services, not being also in Civil employment.

III. The Prizes shall be awarded as follows:—that of £16 to the Boy whom, at the annual Examination in the Junior Grade among Male Candidates qualified in the manner expressed in the next preceding Rule, the Board shall adjudge to rank highest in answering; One Prize of £10 to the Boy whom in the same Grade at such Examination the Board shall adjudge to rank second among such persons in answering; and the other of £10 to the Girl whom, at such Examination in the same Grade, among Female Candidates qualified in the manner aforesaid, the Board shall adjudge to rank highest in answering.

IV. The decision of the Board shall be final and decisive in determining whether the Candidates fulfil the conditions of the third Rule.

V. The Board may deduct all expenses connected with the trust from the yearly income.

No. 4931.

DUBLIN CASTLE,

21st *March*, 1896.

GENTLEMEN,

I have to acknowledge the receipt of your letter of the 20th instant, forwarding, for submission to His Excellency the Lord Lieutenant, the Annual Report of the Intermediate Education Board for Ireland for the year 1895.

I am,

Gentlemen,

Your obedient Servant,

(Signed) D. HARREL.

The Assistant Commissioners of

Intermediate Education,

1, Hume Street, Dublin.